WE EMPOWER

A COLLECTION OF EMPOWERING STORIES FROM WOMEN WHO WERE COURAGEOUS ENOUGH TO HEAL THEIR EMOTIONAL TRAUMA WOUNDS AND NOW HELP OTHERS DO THE SAME

NOSHIELA MAQSOOD

Copyright © 2023 by Noshiela Maqsood

ISBN13 Paperback: 9798387741913

All rights reserved.

No part of this book may be reproduced in any form or by any electronic or mechanical means, including information storage and retrieval systems, without written permission from the author, except for the use of brief quotations in a book review.

CONTENTS

Introduction Noshiela Maqsood	5
About the Author	21
1. THE WAR WITHIN Amrin Razak	23
About the Author	45
2. I AM MORE THAN PEOPLE'S OPINIONS - HOW FINALLY ACCEPTING MYSELF CHANGED MY LIFE. Anieela Arshad	47
About the Author	65
3. ASSALAMUALAIKUM, I AM HAJAR. Hajar Abdul Hamid	67
About the Author	87
4. THE LIGHT AT THE END OF THE LONGEST TUNNEL Mahira Hasanovic	89
About the Author	104
5. WELCOME HOME! THE HOME I'VE BEEN SEARCHING FOR HAS ALWAYS BEEN WITHIN ME Mazada Ahmed, Self-love Queen, United Kingdom	106
About the Author	115
6. FREEDOM FROM THE SHACKLES OF SOCIETY Salma Zhaid	117
About the Author	136
7. NO RISK, NO MAGIC! Sanam Hussain	138

About the Author	163
8. THE PILGRIMAGE WITHIN Umm Sadiq	165
About the Author	183

INTRODUCTION
NOSHIELA MAQSOOD

In the name of Allah, the most merciful.

Welcome to The Empowered Muslimah Collective.

A huge congratulations and thank you to all of these incredible women who committed to their inner healing and turned their pain into power to help others heal and become empowered too. The determination and courage each one of them has shown are inspirational. Be prepared to have the breakthrough you've been waiting for.

When women heal together, we become a powerful force, leading our homes and communities and empowering others to flourish and thrive in life.

> "Amazing is the affair of the believer. Verily all of his affairs are good and this is not for anyone except the believer. If something good happens to him, he is grateful and that is good for him. If something harmful befalls him, he is patient and that is good for him."

Muhammad, peace be upon Him.

Although I learned this hadith when I was nineteen, I was only able to experience this in my own life ten years later. Going through struggles can make us stronger and wiser. When we trust that Allah has our back, seek support and stay in a state of gratitude, blessings will unfold for us in miraculous ways.

When we focus on the positives in our life and learn to navigate through our struggles with trust in Allah, life becomes fruitful.

We Empower is a collection of stories from women sharing their experiences, knowledge and expertise. All of these women have been through life experiences that have led them to heal their trauma wounds and find their purpose in helping others become emotionally empowered.

Our mission is to

Empower Muslim Women to Heal their emotional trauma wounds so they can thrive with purpose and become generational change-makers. I believe we all have a purpose which often gets buried under life's challenges, unresolved emotions and pain. When you heal from the past, you will have the ability to turn your pain into power and start living life true to your purpose. I pray you heal, grow, evolve and empower others. Ameen.

We value

FAITH

All roads lead back to Allah.

FAMILY

Where life is celebrated and love is cherished.

LOVE

With love, we can heal faster and bring joy to the lives of others.

PASSION

Your passion is a sign from Allah. Passion is what makes what we do enjoyable.

CHILDHOOD DREAMS

Fulfil your dreams. Be the person that looks back and says Alhamdulilah, I did it! Follow your dreams and leave your fears behind

LEGACY

What legacy are you creating? How can you impact generations to come?

We value YOU

Being one of our readers, wherever you are in the world, we value and appreciate you. I pray you benefit from this book and would love to see you in our programmes

If you would love to be a part of The Empowered Muslimah Collective and would love to be a part of the legacy we are creating, see the options below.

The Empowered Muslimah Academy:

A safe, trauma-informed space specifically created to support Muslim women on their journey of healing their emotional traumas so they can thrive and live life with passion and purpose. Join the sisterhood so you can heal and thrive with other Muslim women. We aim to heal hearts and strengthen minds.

The pillars of The Empowered Muslimah Academy are:

- Mental health
- Emotional Empowerment
- Spirituality/heart intelligence
- Trauma healing

Certified Coaching Training for Muslim women:

Now more than ever is the best time to start your online coaching business. This is where passion and purpose meet and it is the most rewarding way to earn a halal income, by helping others ease their load.

You can find certified training in:

NLP (Neuro-Linguistic Programming)

Time Line Therapy®

Hypnotherapy

Emotional Empowerment Coaching

Trauma-informed Coaching.

All of these tools and knowledge combined will allow you to help yourself, your loved ones and your clients at the deepest level.

Everything you've experienced in life has had a part to play in the woman you are today. The way you think, behave and communicate is all linked to your world view and your world-view is mainly formed in your early years of life. To be able to live a life you love, you've got to be willing to face your emotional trauma wounds. The more we suppress and hide our emotional baggage, the more likely it will come out as an explosion rather than an expression. Often, the people dearest to us suffer the consequences of our unresolved emotions and trauma.

Thank you for choosing to take time out of your schedule to be a part of my world for a short while. Life can get so busy that often we forget to prioritise ourselves.

Being a mum of five children, the eldest aged ten years and the youngest just seven months, running my coaching and training business as well as the 101 other things on my list - including writing this book - I can tell you that life Is fun!!

I never thought I'd say that! Waking up in the morning and feeling grateful daily for my life is something I never thought would happen. The last ten years have been one heck of a roller-coaster but the fact that I get to empower Muslim women all around the world, write books, become a bestselling author three times over, appear on T.V and radio for my works, be nominated for awards and make a lot of money doing what I love whilst I change nappies, keep my house clean and cook beautiful food for my family, is more than I asked for. I am truly grateful, Alhamdulilah.

The truth is, this didn't happen overnight. There have been some lows, some really low times in my life, and I believe they were all preparing me for the woman I am today and everything that Allah has blessed me with. If you're someone that needs help to start loving life again, to start feeling more confident and emotionally empowered, you're in the right place at the right time. I have something special for you.

Have you ever felt like you've lost passion and excitement in life because your past experiences are weighing heavy on your mind and heavy in your body, holding you back from doing things you love and experiencing life as you should? I know we often hear that life is a test and it is. This doesn't

INTRODUCTION

mean life isn't to be enjoyed, and that we need to get through it miserably. You know, more than anyone in your life, it's Allah that wants you to be happy, to enjoy life and to live by your purpose.

I used to believe that life wasn't supposed to be fun and it was just about obeying commands and doing what we're 'supposed' to, according to the expectations of our parents. I always measured life by a timeline - that I had to do certain things by a certain age, for example, study, get a job, get married, have children and so on. I'm sure many people had the same mindset and many still do! The problem with following set timelines is that we never know what the future holds and most of the time, it's not meaningful to us. I'm a great believer in planning what we want to do, be, have and experience in life without being attached to the outcome because ultimately, Allah is the best planner. We plan and Allah plans. Indeed Allah is the best planner.

I love how my life has turned out, alhamdulilah, but if you had spoken to me six years ago, my version of life was filled with heartbreak, hurt, betrayal and anger. I had lost my passion for living. I was in a dark place and there were many things that led to me being there. I would wake up thinking 'not another day', 'not again', and 'please, Allah, just end this for me' and I genuinely meant it. Even though I was a mum of three beautiful children, I had accomplished some cool things like working at a radio station, leading charity projects and working my dream jobs, I was just at the point in my life where I was craving to go back to doing those things and being the old me. Having children and becoming a stay-at-home mum really threw me. Even though I loved my children dearly, I often felt like I had no purpose in life. Every day would feel the same, doing the same things over and over again, feeling like there was no time for me. I was constantly doing things for everyone else but myself. I neglected myself. I missed the extremely confident version of me. I didn't recognise the way I looked and sounded. I was so bitter and carried a lot of resentment. It was only after I sought professional help and hired a coach, things started to make sense. I told my coach what I was struggling with and how I needed help in my marriage and help to recover from what I felt were the most heartbreaking and mentally draining experiences.

The deeper I went into my healing journey, the more I began connecting the dots back to my childhood. Most people's problems aren't their actual problems, they are a result of deeper issues that haven't been addressed and resolved. The more I began to understand and heal, rather than finding the old me, I felt like I was becoming my true self.

What is it in your life that you feel is holding you back from truly experiencing life?

Have you ever felt like you lost yourself in being there for others?

Do you struggle with maintaining healthy boundaries and end up feeling completely exhausted because you prioritised

INTRODUCTION

everyone else but yourself?

You are not alone. There are so many women that go through similar experiences. Some decide to seek help and overcome their internal and external obstacles. I have coached many women and I have seen them evolve. It's the most beautiful transformation to witness and be a part of.

Through my academy, coaching workshops, trauma-informed coaching certifications for Muslim women and one-to-one coaching and therapy service, I empower women to break trauma cycles and start living in the now rather than reliving the past. I'm passionate about helping Muslimahs become emotionally empowered and financially independent. When we learn how to manage our emotions and regulate our nervous system, we're able to achieve the success we desire in all areas of our lives.

Once you heal and become empowered, you can be there for others without sacrificing your own well-being.

There are three keys to becoming emotionally empowered and financially independent:

1. Self-reflection: Become aware of what needs to change in your life. Which area of your life are you struggling with the most?
2. Self-initiated action: Have the courage to seek professional help and heal from the things that are

bothering you and stopping you from enjoying life and achieving your dream goals.
3. Success roadmap: Turn your pain into power and start living life with purpose. Once you heal, you can start helping others and create an income at the same time.

Here are some ways you can work with me to heal your emotional trauma wounds and start thriving instead of surviving!

The Empowered Muslimah Academy

The academy is a safe, compassion-filled healing space for Muslim women to heal, grow and evolve. It is my signature, trauma-informed, deep-healing program and it consists of:

1. Setting intentions for becoming the best version of you
2. Understanding your thoughts, emotions and behaviours
3. Learning about trauma: what is it? How it affects you mentally, emotionally and physically
4. How to heal from trauma
5. Inner child healing
6. Forgiveness: for yourself and others
7. Eliminating disempowering beliefs that you created about yourself as a result of trauma
8. How to become Empowered

INTRODUCTION

9. Creating a life you love.

The Academy is for you if you want to be supported and guided with Islamic principles and values at the centre of your healing process.

Trauma-Informed Emotional Empowerment Coaching Certification

I truly believe that your calling comes from your trauma. I have had the honour of coaching women who have then gone on to train with me and start their own coaching businesses. Alhamdulilah.

When a woman heals, she heals those around her and the generations to come. If you would love to start a career in coaching and empowering others, this is for you.

My coaching certifications focus on these pillars:

1. Spirituality
2. Emotional Empowerment
3. Trauma healing
4. Neuro-Linguistic programming

After women train with me, they are certified in the following:

NeuroLinguistic programming : (NLP) is the art and science of helping people achieve their desired outcomes by rewiring their minds to change their behaviour. NLP accelerates a person's healing results as it holds the most powerful and dynamic mindset and emotional mastery tools. NLP helps with anxiety treatment, phobias, disorders and so much more

Timeline Therapy practitioner: Time Line Therapy allows you to work with a client to release negative emotions from the root cause without re-traumatising the client. It's easy, quick and powerful and has had life-changing effects on myself and my clients.

Hypnotherapy: is worldwide recognised and known for helping people to get the results they want in life by accessing their unconscious mind to release negative thoughts and emotions, replacing them with positive suggestions.

Trauma-informed coaching: Being trauma-informed allows you to help yourself and your clients to release trauma from the physical body as well as the mind. Often, coaches and therapists work with the mind only, which leaves people with an incomplete solution. You see, the mind is a place where people go to avoid the pain they feel in their body. The pain and tension a person carries within their body is unresolved trauma. Your body has memory. Trauma is never the event or the thing that happened to you, trauma is the imprint it leaves within your body as a result of what happened. There are many different types of trauma and the impact it leaves on a person varies from person to person. This affects every part of your life. Being trauma-informed will change the way you live your life, it will change the way you view other people's behaviours and it will help you to help your loved ones and clients too.

Break the trauma cycle and heal the generations to come.

Here are some testimonials from my clients who worked with me to heal their own emotional traumas and went on to train with me to start their own profitable, passion-led coaching businesses.

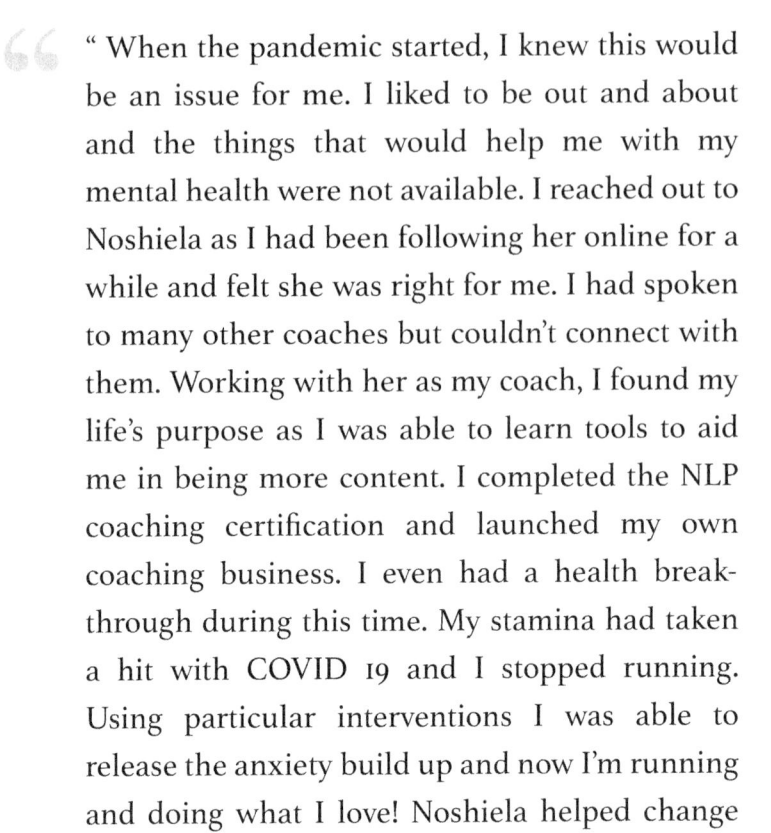

" When the pandemic started, I knew this would be an issue for me. I liked to be out and about and the things that would help me with my mental health were not available. I reached out to Noshiela as I had been following her online for a while and felt she was right for me. I had spoken to many other coaches but couldn't connect with them. Working with her as my coach, I found my life's purpose as I was able to learn tools to aid me in being more content. I completed the NLP coaching certification and launched my own coaching business. I even had a health breakthrough during this time. My stamina had taken a hit with COVID 19 and I stopped running. Using particular interventions I was able to release the anxiety build up and now I'm running and doing what I love! Noshiela helped change 2020 from the year of restrictions to the year of becoming."

— CLIENT R

" I love having Noshiela as my coach, she has a lovely energy that always gets you on a high when you're discussing future goals. From women that need help with deep-rooted emotional traumas to women that want to regularly work on their mindset, Noshiela helps them

INTRODUCTION

all. She's passionate about her coaching and is always taking new courses herself to improve her services. My energy has always been through the roof after having a session, in fact, I was stuck writing a chapter for a book and after my session with her, I completed the chapter. Mindset is something that needs to be consistently worked on and I've always thoroughly enjoyed my work with Noshiela"

— CLIENT S

"I never realised the value of a coach until I worked with Noshiela. There was so much I had to deal with that I didn't realise until I decided to face myself with Noshiela's support. She was sent to me by Allah at the perfect time. She helped me regain my self-belief and confidence and is helping me become the best version of me. After my personal healing journey, I trained with her to become a certified coach and it is the best training course I've ever done. So excited to help so many women change their lives for good!"

— CLIENT S.H

"Having coaching and therapy with Noshiela has been life-changing. Sometimes, talking to someone can help you to feel better but when there's deep-rooted trauma, you need to work with someone who can help you release what you've been holding on to for years. That's exactly what I did. Not only did I heal, but I was also able to get to my core and realise my life's purpose. I feel like dark clouds have been lifted from above my head and now I have so much to look forward to. I can now use these techniques on myself and my loved ones!"

— CLIENT R.A

There are countless testimonials from women who have saved their marriages, reconnected with their children, healed their emotional traumas and found their purpose in helping others.

This can be you too. You have the power to turn your life around by saying yes to yourself.

About the Author
NOSHIELA MAQSOOD

Noshiela provides coaching, training, and transformational events for Muslim women around the world to help them become generational changemakers and thought leaders. Her mission is to empower and support women to empower themselves and embrace their true potential – beyond their pain.

As a certified Trauma-informed NLP trainer, hypnotherapy trainer and emotional empowerment coach for Muslim women all around the world, Noshiela's passion is in helping Muslim women process through the hurt and pain of the past and build lives of purpose, passion and success.

She is a three times best-selling author, a finalist for the "she" awards, a radio presenter and a public speaker. She has appeared on numerous tv channels and interviewed on BBC radio, radio ikhlas and many other popular stations to celebrate and recognise the work she's doing to empower women.

Noshiela is an expert in emotional empowerment and leads women to transform their lives through the power of mindfulness and neurolinguistic science with Islamic principles at the forefront.

I would love to hear from you and have you join The Empowered Muslimah Collective: Healing to thrive

For more information on any of the courses mentioned, check out my website:

www.noshielanoorcoaching.co.uk

Join my free group:

https://www.facebook.com/groups/empoweredmuslimah

Email: noshielanoorcoaching@gmail.com

 facebook.com/noshiela
 instagram.com/noshiela.noor.training.academy

CHAPTER 1
THE WAR WITHIN
AMRIN RAZAK

It's poetic, where I am now. I'm not where I thought I would be. It would have been a very different chapter and book twelve years ago, that's for sure. I couldn't have planned it better myself. There was definitely a divine intervention! All I know is I'm here now on this journey to myself, out of my comfort zone, healing each day. I challenge myself daily, no matter what it is, or how nominal, I focus on being at my highest present self. You know that actual buzz - have you ever experienced that? That natural oxytocin thinking how far you've come, praise be to God? These are highs of contentment, of being fulfilled, of knowing I'm far closer to my life's goals in working with women to find their true identity and purpose through healing childhood traumas and generations of pain. I support them in becoming who they want to and need to be - wholesome women, ultimately coming home to themselves just like I have. I know this is exactly where I'm meant to be too, just like you can.

I'm so proud of the opportunities I've had in the last five years or so. I've travelled across five different countries, which I never thought I would do on my own, especially as a practising hijabi Muslim woman. I'll always cherish the memories of walking the lands where my ancestor and relations bared their struggles and called home. Hoping to one day return, they stood against the oppression and with the economic migration, going through famine and poverty they did their best. Can you imagine? It was a true honour and privilege for me to be there.

I swam in rivers, waterfalls, streams and oceans I'd only dreamed of before. I didn't know how much I loved the water and being in the mountains and the wilderness. I was in my element. I tasted herbs and foraged fruits I'd never seen, let alone been able to harvest. It was a paradise I never imagined. I actually tasted delicacies that were divine, grown and nurtured from the land I walked. I met with some amazing soul sisters who have been some of my biggest fans - my sisters who I'm ever so grateful for. It was on those trips that my path became obvious. It's fundamental to find your tribe of empowered, God-conscious women who are also striving every day.

I'm so appreciative I completed my psychology and counselling degree, which took me six years to do. I'm glad I never then gave up - with God's permission - Islamic sciences, which was a challenge. It was an ongoing battle within myself for years. I am now continuing my studies in scholastic studies in Spiritual Counselling - Oh, and from 2018 to now, I've been working on my coaching business, to support women to heal.

For me, my day starts off around 5 am, with me having a gratitude-to-attitude mindset. I journal, I pray and never stop thanking the Almighty. I go for walks in the morning or have a one-to-one client session with one of my awesome women who want change, who have trusted me to support them to heal, nourish and grow.

I always make time for a coffee, chai and chat, or a book to read - it's the little things that have the biggest impact. I spend many moments playing with my cat, BibiAnnah - yes, I'm a cat mum. She's helped me a lot over the last two years and given me so much joy and love - those who have pets will understand. I work remotely and have restarted working in-person across the city, so there are no two days the same. I absolutely love that I'm in control of how much I choose to do. I'm able to determine what my day needs to be and balance my home life with my commitments to fill my cup. I prioritise what I need physically, emotionally, spiritually and mentally, depending on where I am in my season.

The biggest success is being able to do what I need to do not just for myself but for all the things that complete my world. In the last three years or so, I've picked up cycling again - I hadn't been on a bike for such a long time. I'm in training for a marathon, which has been a goal for so long and this is the year it's going to happen. I picked up art again, being creative, writing, singing, poetry, learning instruments and working on book collaborations and projects. I'm learning Islamic calligraphy and understanding the theology and history behind it all.

I'm an advocate for having wholesome, home-cooked nutritious food. I'm all for eating homegrown, organic foods, free from chemicals as everything we consume has a huge effect on our nervous system and spiritual growth. And by "consume", I mean what we eat, listen to, our immediate circle and our overall environment, which was the deal-breaker when I was in a job that left me unable to commit to my health and spiritual growth. It was something I'd never been able to do before working for myself.

I am able to support my community, which is a huge part of who I am and what I need. The flexibility to arrange weekends away, as and when I need to, just being able to breathe in nature, not being part of the rat race anymore. I'm part of women's walking groups writing and poetry programs, mental health programs, in-person coaching workshops and many other support groups in my locality empowering my community both online and in person.

It's all about how I can be an empowered Muslimah, living my best life - not just for today, it is for the long term and the next life, God willing. I see no other way for me to be and I will continue to be this way in the future, God willing.

WAKE UP CALL

From the age of nineteen, I worked for other organisations. In most roles, I was in the corporate world or charity sector, which was very masculine, looking back. It was go, go, go, sales, targets, getting the next bid, event management, project undertaking - all very highly stressful jobs, working for someone else. I realised a long time ago that it wasn't really filling my cup. It wasn't doing anything for my soul. Yes, I had a great job. Yes, I was travelling up and down the country and sometimes abroad, setting up departments, training, programming and managing, and it paid a good salary that came with some perks, yet I was empty. I was literally running in a meaningless direction and I could best describe it as being a zombie.

HANGING BY A THREAD

Then, in 2010, I experienced grief. I lost my mother after a long battle with illnesses, something I don't wish having to witness upon anyone. Unfortunately, it's the reality that trauma and guilt come with grief. It took me to a point where there was only one way to go - a major breakdown. It just spiralled into a depression where I didn't feel anything for a while. As I was in a robotic state on anti-depressants for some time, any emotions I had were being buried, even if I tried to deal with my pain. The anti-depressants did the job for a short while but I knew something had to change. All I know is I just wanted to feel, for the ache to fade away from me so I could breathe freely!

Then, in 2012, I was briefly married. The marriage was short-lived for many reasons. Being the empath that I was, I wanted to save everyone and be a saviour. Can you imagine being so empty yourself and then trying to support someone who also had so much of their own trauma that hadn't been dealt with? I went through a lot in that year of my life. I changed jobs, country, home, friends, everything. My whole life turned upside down in the pursuit of happiness and contentment. You know, the remnants of this kind of pain, vulnerability, mental illness, health, financial and spiritual abuse never ever just leaves you. This may resonate with those of you reading this. I was really naive. I was vulnerable because of grief and anguish. I was trying to fill the void, of darkness within myself, having high false expectations that it could be filled by a marriage. Ultimately, I was looking in all the wrong places just to feel a connection.

Within our cultures, we're taught that as women, you put everything into other people - especially the men in your life, as in spouses, fathers, uncles, or brothers. It's not wrong, but it is when you forget yourself in the bigger picture of your own life. We're not taught the tools to deal with life's journey and thirty-something years of insecurity, people pleasing, colourism, body shaming, heightism, abandonment issues, generational trauma, spiritual bypassing and unhealthy relationship and bad opinions of God are the result.

The universe, as I understood it, just didn't make sense anymore. I knew this wasn't it, I knew that this life was only a prison for those who don't live it in line with God's commandments. The hopeful, optimistic person that I am now, chose to change the narrative, not be a victim. When this episode came to a close, all I remember is feeling saved, covered in a blanket of love, compassion and mercy. It felt as though a weight had been lifted and I was not hanging by a thread anymore. My God made it really easy for me to walk away, and I was safe - now and in every situation that I have been faced with since. Twelve years ago, I made a vow to heal, nourish and grow, and to bring other women to pave their own journey to return home and to finally:

 "Create your Own Beautiful"

LOVE IN YOUR PAIN

After this experience, I took six months or so to go travelling, which was the life-changing experience I so craved and needed... Nobody expected I would go travelling after being married, least of all me! I was the timid, shy type and not as independent as I thought when I was growing up. Well, that's what I thought until my thirties. In this soul's journey back to the self. I went to war-torn countries, across the far east, borders, Africa, Jungles, remote tribal Islands and into

Europe. I went supporting in orphanages, schools, safe houses, hospitals, camps and farms across the world! The fact is, it was what my soul was crying out for and I finally had a soul-shattering awakening. As a culture and society, we live in we think when we give to charity or give our time to support people, donating things that we're the ones doing "Good" for others, right? No. In fact, we're the ones in need of good deeds to weigh heavily on our scales, when it matters to get us through this life. Seeing these sights reminded me the only war I was fighting was within myself.

After being on this journey to the self, I started to fall back into unhealed traumas. I thought I was healing, so I threw myself back into a new job the perfect role that met my values and fulfilled me... for a while. I thought I'd been fixed and was ready to take on the world, only to realise I'd done the short-term work but not the long-term mindset shifts that were needed. I found I was falling into relationships - be it professional or personal - where I was being triggered and left feeling deflated with unmet needs and no boundaries set. It didn't make sense to me. I thought I was filling my cup but I was starting to feel similar traumas coming up from past experiences.

The reason it happened is I lost focus on myself and what I needed. I wasn't present in my life and so it just became a checklist to tick off and repeat the next day. I sincerely advise, whatever you're doing, if it's not in line with your vision and goals then stop, or you'll be back ten steps, always playing catch up and going to war against yourself. I say "Divine truth is to free yourself from the self". That is the grandest of challenges. I was trying to fulfil what I thought I needed, but I was not of a sound heart and mind and so I was constantly doubting myself and second-guessing, seeking that approval.

The advice, looking back is to look at the signs. See what's going on internally. Check in every day and look at where you are on a physical, spiritual and mental level. Look at your physiology, your food intake and of course, how in sync you are with your moon cycle. Recognise if you're getting pains in your body, for example, if you're not sleeping well or you're agitated, anxious or you're binge eating, as these are messages for you. Next look at how present you are with the relationships around you, your close-knit circle. Are people starting to pick up on things? How are your communication skills? Are you short with people and not giving them time? Look at that.

What is your relationship with your creator? Who are you at your best and your worst? Who are you in your silence? What is your internal dialogue? Are you self-aware? How do you show up? How does that affect those around you on a day-to-day basis and those who meet you once?

Where are these thoughts and behaviours coming from? For me, I thought I was doing all the right things because I needed a salary and I needed to be in a job. I believed so much in what I was doing that even if someone told me to my face that I was sabotaging and working from a place of unhealed trauma, I wouldn't have believed it.

I guess in hindsight, I just wanted to be part of something bigger than myself and didn't think I could ever have my own dreams. I now know this was a trend in all my trauma responses to life circumstances. Always remember, you can only belong when you are a completely wholesome woman yourself first. Ensure that you're looking at what you're doing to fill yourself - and I don't mean from a self-centred or superficial point of view. I mean it from a self-care and love perspective. It's about getting the balance right And making sure that you're not sabotaging yourself.

My self-sabotaging actions became my default world view and I was fast spiralling into burn-out. Eventually, I got to a point where I just thought "I don't want to do this anymore". I realised that was the same thought I had when I left what I was doing previously. It hit me - "I'm not serving myself, let alone anyone else right now". I was conflicted, I didn't recognise who I'd become - the people-pleasing, wanting to belong, being harsh with people because of my own frustrations, having someone breathing down my neck, sky-high stress levels... It became so bad that I didn't know myself anymore. It may sound unreal but I didn't recognise myself in the mirror. That was because my lack of self-confidence and all those insecurities I had ten years ago hadn't really gone away.

I knew I was really playing small. I thought it was an opportunity, just like those in the past. I now realise, looking back, that I took the role because I felt it was within my comfort zone. Even then, no matter how much I did, it was never enough, just like some of my relationships in the past. I've since learnt that even when an opportunity comes, just breathe and ensure to check your intentions and purpose. Is it going to facilitate your journey beyond yourself? If you're conflicted then look deeper. Don't forget to reassess and check in with your soul. Speak to those who you can seek the right advice from, whether it's about work, setting up a project, a small business... whatever it is. Of course, have a conversation with God - never stop that regardless of where you are in your daily obligations. Ensure it is consistent and compatible with you - that's fundamental, that's key. The point is, sometimes, just because you're given the opportunity, it doesn't mean to say it's the right opportunity. Ultimately, saying "No," takes more courage. Stay in your lane and master it. As Muslims, we are taught to believe in predestination, so whatever is for you will come around again and won't miss you when everything is aligned.

JUST SURVIVING TO THRIVING

In this journey of life I recognised that I wasn't content. I was doing the external work, as in I was busy being busy, however, I was not doing all the internal work because that was scary, I didn't know how. I knew that I needed healing, but I was so exhausted and I was so drained. I wasn't able to heal or even make the right choices to find a coach or teacher. I was just running blindly, it seemed, so I was barely surviving. I can only describe it as literally hanging by a thread. Then, something changed. I don't know what but it was a lightning bolt moment. I have no idea who or where it came from, whose prayers, or if the angels said "Aameen" but something shifted.

As believers, we must recognise that God teaches us duality through everything he's created, therefore there have to be opposites, so when we're faced with good people, there are also bad people, in order to see the morning dawn, we must worship the night. All situations and events provide wisdom and lessons to apply.

I can only describe it as just as I felt like nobody was coming to save me, my Creator, a Divine Presence, the Master Planner sent me a line to pull me out of that, deep, drowning hole.

It took time. For a long while, I did not recognise myself. I avoided connecting with people on a personal deep level, not getting too deep, not letting my guard down, because then disappointment would follow., This was the opinion I had of human beings and I just wanted to protect myself.

There were so many moments when I would come home and I would be totally exhausted. I would literally collapse on my bed or floor whatever I could get to first. Your home is supposed to be your sanctuary, right? But I'd bring work home with me, so there was never an off switch. I wasn't doing anything for myself, for my own self-healing or nurturing. I was giving out a lot, but I wasn't doing any self-care or self-love. I didn't know how to receive - only now, after twelve years of my healing journey, have I learned. I was so immersed in everything else that I was just doing and not actually being.

At the time, I didn't get it and I developed such an abrasive manner. During this period of my life, my responses were stress induced and my tone was harsh at times, even though it was not intentional. I had been that harsh to myself for years. Close friends started to comment."You're not smiling, you're not laughing," they said, " What's happened?". People I hadn't seen in a while would say "You don't look like your bright, normal self. You look exhausted," or, "we haven't seen you for so long". These comments really hit home and I realised this really wasn't what I wanted. It was not fulfilling what I wanted long-term and I realised I was either isolating or self-sabotaging, depending on the situation. I knew it wasn't serving me. I literally had a burnout, along with anxiety attacks, stress-induced stomach reflux, insomnia, weight gain... I tried to keep ignoring these issues as there was so much going on, both on a global level and also in my personal life.

It was just before my 40th birthday. I was not happy with who I was. I'd allowed my Insecurities and my own self-talk and self-hate to rule. Instead of being angry or upset at the situation, I decided I would not block it out again and I started making changes. They were small, but they were significant and consistent changes. I started self-learning. I started looking into my driving force, re-evaluating my coping mechanisms and why I behaved the way I did, through the temperaments framework. I started looking into my own trauma responses - what I do when I'm at my worst, my self-sabotage patterns and understanding my love languages. I started reading up and cleared my social media of anything that wasn't helping, or that fuelled my anxieties. I searched for support in my professional development. I invested any savings into myself by getting a proper coach to help me with my healing journey.

I started to go for walks again. I started to see daylight. I started to eat healthier. I got a naturopath coach. I started to connect with people that I hadn't connected with in a long while. That part of my whole life for the last five years or so had been a bit of a blur with parts missing.

HINDSIGHT

Looking back now, I tell my younger self to honour herself. I would tell her to know her rights as a Muslim woman and get educated with the right intentions. I would tell her to know that she is worthy, know that every woman is worthy and that she also has a right to have it all - she is the honoured guest. I would not tell her to do this out of ego. I would say to do it out of love and compassion for herself, just as her Maker made her to be. I would tell her that she should not place her trust and fulfilment in others' approval. or on what others perceive of her. I would say don't put yourself last, don't play small, don't settle, and don't sabotage yourself by saying yes to everything, even though they may seem like really great opportunities initially. When something is niggling and starts to feel not quite right, check in with yourself. Know that if something isn't quite right, it's a signal from that innate intuition that God, Mother Nature, the Divine has given you, so tap into it every day. That's what I would say to my younger self and to you.

There are people that will come into your life to teach you lessons you never knew you needed to learn. Not all people are supposed to stay in your life, some are just for a season. It's okay to admit you could have done better. Make a commitment to do better for yourself first.

Never underestimate the power of your inner healing. It's in times of hardship you realise how far you've come!! Don't take advice from people that haven't walked your path. You, in your heart, know what's best for you, Always put Allah first and pray.

The best thing you can do for yourself is to heal from your emotional trauma wounds, so when you are dealing with a challenging situation, you're able to not only get through it but GROW through it.

My self-healing started five years ago. God knew what I needed and He kept sending me the right people. I mean, I was seeking, I knew there was something more, I knew there was something better but realising that He, God, was making it easy for me was like an epiphany.

A number of things happened at that time. I got in touch with a dear friend that I hadn't seen in such a long time. She had lost her mother and she was going through her own grief. It had been thirteen years since I'd lost my mother but it still resonated. She put me in touch with somebody who is very much a spiritual person and had a psychological background. She supports women to empower themselves through Islamic Counselling. In terms of an Islamic framework, I hadn't come across anyone like that, a female scholar who was well-versed in the sciences and had come highly recommended. I believe that we are sent messengers, through means of His creation, through each other.

We have more power in our lives than we realise. Back in my dark days, remember thinking, I am not happy with the situation that I'm in right now, so what can I do? What can I do to change myself? And I made those changes. I started working from home. I started doing courses to complete the rest of my education alongside further studies into the self and understanding my own childhood trauma and healing. It was what I needed. I wanted to change the story and for that to happen, I needed to heal. As soon as I accepted that, it was so much easier.

And that's when another bolt hit me. I guess because of the resilience I've had and yes, maybe because of my naivety and my trust in people, I always assumed that people wanted the best for me, which is a good opinion to have but you need to be cautious. Not all people are good or are going to be like you, that's the duality of human beings. People have their own ways and ultimately, they'll be answerable for their actions. I'm now okay with that because I understand everyone comes from their own lived experiences, traumas and world view. They come into your life to teach you something.

I'm also certain that, while I believe I am destined for greater, we must always remember, if it's for our ego and to soothe the self, it will never be successful in the long term. My motto is that as a woman, we can heal a nation. And I truly believe that we all have that innate nature within ourselves. This wisdom has been gifted to us. We also need to accept that we never fully heal until we really do put the changes to work with the unconscious mind. The work must continue, we will always be better-healed women than when we started. It's understanding that we need to give ourselves that time to nurture ourselves, to the way Mother Nature and the Divine have created us to be.

Continuing my studies brought me to this place. I completed my Neuro Linguistic Programming Practitioner certification and Emotional Mastery. I did many other programs and training about how we work with the soul, and our nature but also against our ego. It's an ongoing journey. I now use this knowledge as part of my coaching practice for my clients as I work with women to heal, nourish and grow.

I help them to be wholesome women of God. It doesn't matter where you are or which faith you come from, I believe we all have that Divine light within ourselves. I truly believe now, looking back, that I had to go through my trials - the burnout and unhappiness - to come out of the other side, allowing the light to enter every situation that I faced over the last thirteen years or so.

I don't harbour any blame towards anyone or my upbringing, background, or the adults in my life - they did the best that they could with what they had at the time. I know not everyone is as fortunate as me. At the point where I was so broken, I just said to God, "Just give me what's good for me. I don't know what to do. Just give me certainty, give me something, in all that You want of me so that I can be a good servant and You can be pleased with me. Show me how I can be of service to others, to be all that I can in terms of my passion projects and things that are important to me - the things that align with my values, the things that make me jump out of bed, and give me a buzz or a splurge of inspiration, whether that's to write poetry or to put a journal entry in or design a coaching course".

I asked for something, not knowing what it was, I just knew there was more,! He gave me that power, the superpower that I believe we all have, but not everyone is shown. Once you have knowledge of something, you must act upon it accordingly and use it correctly. As we say with knowledge, it's not to be kept to yourself, it is to be guided or taught. I truly believe that everything has its time. I know ten years ago was not the right time for many things that I thought I needed. I was coming from a wounded place of self-sabotage and unhealed trauma.

PURPOSE IN YOUR POWER

Once you are given your purpose, just like any gift, it's a privilege and honour given to you. You've been crowned and celebrated by the Divine and it is yours to wear, just as I wear my hijab. You are an honoured guest on this path you are walking. You have to nurture and grow your purpose just like a plant pot - it doesn't just become a garden without nurturing, does it? And It's your responsibility now. Five years ago, I never thought I wanted to be a coach. You know, people would say to me Amrin you'd be a really good coach, you're so inspiring, you have a voice and wisdom. I would say "No, I need to do a nine-to-five job that's stable," trying to be humble. I lacked faith in myself. I had this limiting belief that I needed to work for someone else. My language was, "I can't" - I didn't even get to the "How"! I simply said I can't be a coach. I can't. I can't. I can't.

But we are all given tools in our pack and it's what we do with them that matters. Coaching was in my toolkit.It wasn't just one moment that led me here or one awakening. It was many situations and instances, people who I believe were Divine lights were sent to me. It was a snowball effect. So here I am, Yes, I'm still healing as it's a lifelong journey. I'll get curve balls now and again but now I know what my responses will be, it's not traumatic or taking me back to my childhood. I'm able to be in a balanced space, where I'm nurturing myself and I'm using wisdom and knowledge. Now I'm able to empower, influence and nurture not only myself but those around me, my community. I'm able to do this because I'm constantly learning, evolving and maturing. I'm looking through a different lens and discovering how I can improve and better myself and better my services.

It's vital to have mentors and qualified coaches - therapists are not the same. You must have a succinct business model that works with you and for you. I like to be challenged - we all need that for consistent growth. I'm growing and heading in the right direction so I can continue working with women across the world. The women I have worked with are able to have healthy, balanced relationships. They are women who are living their best life in the careers they want, women who now have better relationships with their partners because they're not insecure anymore. They have worked through their insecurities, abandonment issues, hate, resentment, guilt and childhood trauma and now have a greater understanding of their relationships with their parents. They are women who are not going back to the same abusive relationships and making the same trauma-bonded mistakes, mothers whose children don't frustrate them and are better-focused mums with no mum guilt.

I have many plans for the coming years, which I'm really excited about. These plans will ensure I can provide support for even more women to be able to identify how they want to show up through their inner, innate power ultimately, defining who they want to be in the future. I can help them work on their past traumas and limiting beliefs and use these as a superpower in order to heal, nourish and grow and be better-grounded women, able to support and maintain themselves. That equilibrium, that safe inner sanctuary of contentment is the sanctuary and saviour I wish for all women.

I hope that I can continue my journey to supporting more women with my passion and purpose. I have nurtured and supported many women, the testimonials speak for themselves, for which I'm truly honoured and grateful. We all have experiences but we don't have to live with the trauma every waking moment. We don't need to fight fire with fire, barely surviving. Take your pain back to heal you, it does not need to define you - that was you then not now. You're allowed to let go.

I create and curate safe spaces for women to come in, be nurtured, heal their wounds, and work on how they can empower themselves. Be stronger, resilient, feminine women - not from a wounded place but from a divine light, through womb work, inner healing, breath work, energy healing, hypnotherapy, visualisation and finding her true innate voice connecting to the divine presence.

The inner sanctum is just like a garden that needs to be

planted and watered. Give it light, a shade when needed, then clear the weeds out. I support women to be able to do that and create those safe spaces to influence and grow. I provide one-to-one or group sessions, both in the online space and in person. I have done a number of retreats and plan to do many more in the coming years, both here and abroad. I'm supporting my tribe of women to be able to be fully mindful, functioning women, not living in fear.

No matter what their life choices- be it to forge a career or to work as a homemaker, using their innate feminine power, I want women to live a life of abundance and wholeness, to support themselves and ultimately, educate themselves using all the tools from a holistic, faith and spiritual framework. I believe women especially have that divine gift. I support women to be able to connect to themselves through the womb and heart work, so I would like to invite you into my Inner sanctuary of Healed Content Wholesome Women.

Heal | Nourish | Grow

Empowering Muslim Women to Turn Pain into Power

About the Author
AMRIN RAZAK

Amrin lives in the Midlands with her family. She also cares for her father, which is a true blessing. She loves nothing more than a good book she can get lost in. She found her true voice when she took the pen to speak from the heart. She is a spoken word artist and can be seen performing on open mic nights and hosting the space for many other women too. She has set up a Women's Poetic platform named "She Speaks" to allow women to perform their poetic prose on a monthly basis. She is an advocate for supporting women in her community as much as she can. She can be found appearing on local radio discussing women's issues, topics that affect Muslim women today and acquiring a growth mindset.

She loves to learn new things, especially with regard to her business and industry. Across the city, she curates coaching programs to empower women to heal from their trauma and ultimately connect to the divine. She believes "once we choose to transform our pain into a superpower, we can educate a nation to heal, nourish and grow, it's all about what we give our attention to. As women, we have influencing powers and it's using those powers for good intentions, ultimately to return home."

I look forward to connecting.

CHAPTER 2
I AM MORE THAN PEOPLE'S OPINIONS - HOW FINALLY ACCEPTING MYSELF CHANGED MY LIFE.

ANIEELA ARSHAD

There are so many small moments in my day that I am now grateful for because they are moments I never really thought I would have. I am happy and peaceful in myself. The noise that was there isn't there anymore, and that is one of the best things to come from the last three years of focusing on myself

Truly accepting myself and knowing my worth was the starting point for everything else. For me, it means I respect myself so much more, and people-pleasing isn't an issue anymore. I can give my opinion on something without overthinking and worrying about the outcome. The way I look at my life, relationships and work has completely shifted.

Assalaamu Alaikum, I'm Anieela, your self-acceptance coach. I am a mum to two beautiful boys, aged ten and seven. I run a coaching practice helping Muslim women find love, peace and acceptance from within. It has been a whirlwind of a journey, filled with lots of tears and laughter.

My biggest successes are my sons and the relationship I have with them. I know what could have been if I didn't take the time to work on myself and deal with the emotional baggage I was carrying for so long.

Life has its ups and down for us all. I am grateful to Allah that I can understand that there are lessons in everything and I no longer have to worry and obsess about being the perfect mum, wife, and daughter-in-law. Allah created me as I am. I am grateful for that and I do the best I can. There was a time this seemed impossible.

If there is one thing I could tell the teenage version of me it would be this:

Accept yourself as you are and know that you are worthy!! You are good enough; you are loved and by the will of Allah, you can achieve anything you want. Focus on what you want for yourself without comparing yourself to others. It took me what feels like forever to realise this, and when I finally did, one of my first thoughts was to wonder why I hadn't seen it sooner.

The reason I didn't was that my mindset was wired completely differently. For as long as I can remember, others' expectations and opinions weighed heavily on me. I felt like I didn't fit in anywhere. In trying to fit in, somewhere along the line I started thinking that if others were happy with me, I would be happy and find my place.

I was a serial people-pleaser. I would often go out of my way for others without thinking of my own needs and I found it hard to say no. Deep down, all I really wanted was to feel good about myself. It felt good to be appreciated and acknowledged and to feel like I was seen. The thing was, the more I was pleasing others, the more I worried about what they thought of me. Internally, I held the belief that they knew me better than I knew myself. This meant I would go along with things because they were right and I was wrong.

I was probably in Year 9 when I had the idea that I would fake it until I made it. I didn't feel happy within myself or very confident, clever or pretty, so I would just fake it. I put on a mask of fake confidence and happiness, painted on a smile and off I went, thinking that somehow if I faked it for long enough, it would become reality. Are you someone who does this, do you fake it until you make it?

The combination of all these things started a whirlwind of overwhelm and overthinking for me. When you focus on others so much, you are not focusing on yourself and you begin to lose sight of who you are, and what makes you happy. It becomes a vicious cycle.

I would overthink even the smallest of things, things that were nothing to someone else. I would sit and analyse, why this happened and why I said that. I believed other people thought I was an idiot. Some evenings, I would sit and wonder what was wrong with me. Allah had truly blessed me with so much - amazing parents and a loving family. I knew how blessed I was so it didn't make sense to me why I felt this way. I began to feel guilty for not being more grateful and for feeling such negativity inside me.

I was living on autopilot, just getting through the day, ticking off the to-do list and just going through the motions. I felt there was something wrong with me. Why couldn't I just get it together? I wanted more for myself; I just didn't know what.

I had spent so much time faking it that I ended up wanting to be someone else. I didn't like who I was inside. I didn't feel good enough and it felt like something was missing in my life. I wanted to be someone who was happy and at peace internally and externally, doing something I loved and enjoying the simple, fun things in life. I had no idea that the path that Allah had put me on was leading to exactly that. Alhumdulillah.

All I wanted was to be confident. I thought that would fix it all. I wasn't aware at the time that what I needed was to understand myself and my emotions better. To change the way I was looking at things and accept myself for who I was. Confidence goes deeper than we realise. At the heart of it, you have to have a balance of self-acceptance, self-worth, self-esteem and emotional awareness. This is so you can believe in yourself enough to get through the ups and downs in life and know you are doing the best you can.

I lacked any self-worth and self-esteem so my confidence was non-existent, and I used to hide it well. Alhumdulillah I had so much in my life, and I did feel very blessed with how my life was. My mum has always said that when things don't go your way, still be grateful to Allah for what you have and remember Allah tests those whom He loves. This is what got me through many of the tough times before I learned anything about personal development.

The thing I struggled with was I didn't understand why I deserved any of what I had. I carried this with me even when my first son was born. It didn't make sense to me how I was blessed in that way. Have you ever felt like you have so much and hardly anything at all, all at the same time? I was seeing things through a lens of not being worthy enough for anything and that was clouding my judgment about everything.

We carry the experiences of our childhood with us, people are not always aware but these experiences can harm how you see yourself, your relationships, your work and your goals as an adult. At school, I was one of maybe four Asians in a majority-white school. I was the only Muslim girl; the differences were obvious but it took me a while to realise I was different because of my religion as much as my skin colour. I would get racist comments and brush them off. I felt I didn't have the right to be hurt because I was probably being too sensitive. I went along with others to try and fit in but still didn't feel like I did fit in. Another girl could do the same thing as me and that was great but for me, it was a whole other story. Why was I being singled out? I felt like I was being pushed away even more and on top of that, I was blaming myself for it and taking everything to heart. I hated myself for it.

The one moment where so much of the negativity slipped away was when I started wearing hijab, and consciously decided to strengthen my imam. It was my last year of secondary and I just knew it was right for me, I didn't care what anybody said. Yes, I was laughed at and had random comments from girls I thought were my friends but it was one of the greatest times in my life. I had taken a step sincerely for the sake of Allah and I felt amazing, really happy, and confident. But it didn't last. The feeling of not being good enough, not believing in myself and comparing myself to others was still there.

As Muslim women, our faith is central to who we are. Many women assume that if they're struggling emotionally and mentally, the only thing they need to do is pray and make more dua. This is an essential part, but you also have to spend time understanding your emotions and mental health to have peace and enjoy the life that Allah has given you. If internally you feel good about yourself then, the praying, dua, and dhikr are coming from a better place.

I was so happy wearing hijab but I was still so critical of myself and desperate to fit in. When I had my hijab pulled off my head by some girls on the bus - the bus I had taken practically every day to go to college - to me, it was another example of not being good enough, not being seen and not fitting in.

I know many women struggle with this idea of feeling good enough and being seen as good enough. In south Asian culture, this is directly linked to the way you look. So many generations of women have come to think it is normal to be judged and to judge someone else by their appearance, the ideal being tall, slim, and fair.

As a British Pakistani, the label of being "fat" and "not fair enough" has followed me for most of my life. The sad thing is, it just became a normal conversation because everybody was having the same conversations. No one stops to think about the impact it can have on a girl just trying to find her place in life, or how these labels will become part of her beliefs about herself and be carried into her marriage and parenting.

My size and weight felt like it was an issue for many people. I heard conversations about me being too big, that I needed to be thinner or I needed to eat less. I tried every fad diet and would search through magazines for the latest diet and exercise tips. I remember thinking about what would happen if I stopped eating or what if I just ate what I wanted and made myself sick afterwards. I didn't know anything about eating disorders, I just wanted to be thin and fit in with everyone else. The only thing that stopped me was a conversation with my mum, somehow, she realised what I was thinking - call it mothers' intuition, I guess. I will never forget the conversation we had... "Allah has given us food to eat and enjoy and to nourish our bodies. We don't do things that are going to hurt our bodies."

My being "fat" defined who I was. It felt like everyone was judging me because of it, and probably thinking I was an idiot for not being able to lose weight. This was my thought process. I tried to block it out and carry on, but at some point, I started to believe that I was fat and that I was always going to be. I felt constantly deflated, tired from painting a smile, tired from trying to fit in and please others just so I could feel better about myself. None of it made me feel any better. I didn't realise it at the time but my whole identity, my whole idea of being happy had become attached to losing weight and being thin. I would only be happy when I was thin. Are you attaching your happiness to something? Do you tell yourself I'll be happy when...?

Now, I'm going to be honest, I never thought I was that dark-skinned, too dark, needed to be lighter, etc. I was what I like to call a happy medium. But my skin colour was a way I was compared to others. I was judged on it and made to feel less than others. It used to make me angry - really angry - and I couldn't make sense of it. I felt I shouldn't be angry because I was sure the people saying it somehow had my best interest at heart. When you want approval and acceptance from others, you will make excuses for their behaviour and not respect yourself and your boundaries. When you lack boundaries, YOU are the one that suffers.

I didn't know where to direct the anger, so just got angry with myself. There was not one day I didn't think about the food I was eating or that I should be exercising more or eating less. I felt stuck in a black hole, mentally drained, too fat and too dark and always the odd one out.

I thought that when I got married things would change, that suddenly, all the negativity I had felt would melt away. Things don't just go away though, no matter how much you want them to. You have to accept yourself and understand yourself well enough to know what you want and to be happy within yourself, otherwise, you are taking all of that baggage into your marriage and parenting. When you spend a lot much time not valuing yourself, you end up tolerating too much negativity, both from your thoughts and habits and from taking on others' opinions about you.

Through it all, the one thing I focused on was making dua, a lot of it was at my lowest times. I prayed for something to change. After having my oldest son, mum guilt added to the self-criticism, comparing, and feeling worthless. I was anxious all the time and drained from overthinking every possible outcome of something that hadn't even happened. I started getting triggered very easily and would lash out over something small.

The moment I knew I had to change came when my oldest son was around four., We were sat at the kitchen table reading. He was diagnosed with a developmental delay when he was two. It's something we worked through as a family and with all that considered, he was doing well in school. We were sitting reading and he kept mixing up his words and with every word he got wrong I could feel the anger bubbling in me, and I kept pushing it down. All I kept thinking was if you're a good mum you won't shout at him, but he could tell I was getting annoyed. I just wanted to get through it without shouting... it didn't work. After putting him to bed, and giving him extra hugs and kisses because I felt guilty, then I sat at the kitchen table with a cup of tea and just started crying.

I knew he was doing his best, why was I getting annoyed? That was the moment it clicked. It wasn't about him, it was about me. Everything I was feeling, all the negative things I was thinking were being pushed out onto him because I wanted to avoid dealing with it. I was ashamed. Everything that I had bottled up was starting to affect my children and that was the last thing I wanted. I had to find a way for me to be happy again.

I had to ask myself some tough questions. It was the only way things were going to change.

What was happening in my life? I knew I had many blessings in my life, but I was not able to see them clearly because I felt really low about myself. I was tired and overwhelmed and I felt I had to hold it all together because if I didn't, it meant I was a failure.

Why was this happening? I was comparing myself and constantly worrying about what others were thinking. I didn't believe in myself, and I had spent too long faking it, and wanting to be someone else. I was worrying too much about things I could not control. I was blaming others so I didn't have to admit it was me.

What could I change? I wanted to feel more at ease within myself, so that meant looking at what would make me happier. At this time, I still had no idea about personal development, I just did what felt right. I started to exercise a little bit more and eat a little healthier. I would treat myself to a cake or chocolate and try not to feel guilty. I loved art so I got myself a little sketchbook. Skincare was my self-care, I had a set routine, cleanse, tone, moisturise, and add in a face mask now and then. It made me feel really good to have a fresh face.

It was a start and it did make a difference. It allowed me to see I had to focus on myself a little more. But the negative feelings were still there and I didn't know how to make them go away. I joined a network marketing company, hoping that it would distract me from everything else going on. It only made things worse for me but it was the first time I heard about this thing called mindset. I was like wow, what if I apply all this stuff to me, my marriage and my parenting? Things might change for the better! It was around a year or so after that, that I started working with a coach. What I needed was to heal from the past and let go of all the emotional baggage I had been carrying. It was like coming up for air, breathing the freshest of fresh air. The things I never thought would make sense suddenly did. As I healed, I became stronger and was able to connect the dots and let go of so much pain.

One of the most beautiful things I learned along the way is that Allah does not make mistakes so nobody has the right to tell anyone else what they should look like or be like. Remember this the next time you feel low about the way you look. As Muslims, this is something we know, and can easily forget when toxic cultural traits get mixed in with Islam.

By giving myself permission to heal, change and grow, my life started to look like what I had prayed for. All I wanted was to have peace of mind and to enjoy the small moments with my family. I am calmer because I have more clarity about myself and my emotions. My relationships have flourished. I am more present with my children and enjoy spending time with them so much more. I respond rather than react because I understand my emotions better. If I get triggered, I ask myself what is coming up for me it helps calm things down before an overreaction happens. Don't get me wrong, I still have my moments; we are human after all, but I now have a better understanding of myself, my mind is clearer and I use the tools I have to help me. The negative beliefs I had are now gone. I believe in myself more, so I am easier on myself. Something I never thought I would say is that I am proud of myself for every step I have taken.

I have gone from not feeling good about myself to having a coaching business committed to helping Muslim women feel good about themselves.

The starting point to all of this was truly accepting myself. I remember being in a coaching session, we were talking about my health and all the things I had been through with my weight and body image. My coach asked me "Anieela, do you accept yourself?" In my head, I knew that answer was no. I hesitated to say it because I knew it meant I had to change and open another box I had locked tight. I just let go and I said "No, I don't," and I started crying. At that moment, all I felt was relief. I had admitted to the thing I was scared of and now was the time to heal that wound, learn and grow. Allah had shown me a way to change for the better and live my life the way I truly wanted. It was time to trust in that. When you build a house, the core needs to be strong, the foundations need to be right. The foundation of your confidence and resilience and everything else you want is your self-acceptance and self-worth.

Healing your self-acceptance wound allows you to understand how your childhood experiences impact your life right now, and how childhood wounds can take the driver's seat in your relationships, business, and everything that you do. It allows you to connect the dots and understand what needs to change.

There are three key steps to healing your self-acceptance wound. The first is self-assessment, this is what I did when I wanted to make a change in my life. I spoke earlier about how I had to ask myself some uncomfortable questions when I knew I could no longer go on the same.

Self-Assessment is about looking at your life and understanding where you're at - looking at what is happening in your life, and why; understanding what has happened before this, that might be having an impact, and what emotions keep coming up for you. In order to change and be open to the possibilities, you have to take ownership of yourself and your actions. This means being honest with yourself and stepping out of victim mode. When you feel like you are drowning, it's easy to blame others - your parents, husband, in-laws or even your children. The truth is, for you to feel better you have to look within.

Self-forgiveness is the second step. When we talk about forgiveness, there is a belief that we need to forgive others for hurting us to move on. While I agree this is important, the reality is that you have to forgive yourself first. When things are left unresolved, they fester and grow, even when you are trying to bury them. People become angry with themselves. To truly move on, you have to be compassionate with yourself and forgive the choices you have made in the past.

The final step is self-acceptance. This is truly and wholly accepting yourself, after doing all the emotional healing and dealing with the negative emotions and beliefs. Accepting yourself as you are, even if you still have work to do. Part of self-acceptance is prioritising your self-care - accepting that to love and accept yourself from within, you have to take care of yourself mentally, emotionally, and physically.

Here is how you can start the process of your self-assessment. Sit down with a pen and paper and think about the following.

Where am I in my life now?

Where do I want to be?

What's stopping me from having the life I want?

What can I do to regain my power and get my life to where I want?

Be honest with yourself, without judgment. Write down whatever comes to mind, it's okay if it feels less easy. It's meant to because you are starting to look at things differently, go with it and put your trust in Allah. Doing the self-assessment allows you to realise what the problem is, and then you are in a place to move forward.

Finally accepting myself and realising my self-worth allowed me to move on and focus on the future instead of being stuck in the past. So often, when something or someone causes hurt, or anger there is a rush to carry on as normal after the initial outburst of emotion... "I'm over it, it's ok". In truth, it gets buried and pushed to that back burner, only to trigger you again when you are in s similar situation or with similar people. You have to acknowledge it, work through it, and let go.

The things I had experienced growing up led to toxic beliefs about myself which I was finally able to heal from and see that I was worthy of everything I wanted. I have clearer boundaries for what I commit to and what I will tolerate, which is so empowering. I continue to strive to strengthen my Imaan. It is a continuous process and being in control of my emotions allows me to do a better job.

I was always taking things personally, especially in my marriage, because I felt so low. I have dealt with the emotions that were coming up for me and I am aware of my triggers, so things that seemed a massive deal just aren't anymore. I can be a better mum now. Before I was distracted by everything going on in my head. I would get angry quickly and pour shame on myself for the tiniest things. Now I am calmer and more present and the way I talk to my sons is so much better. The best thing about this is that I can see that both my boys are happier and as a mum, there is no better feeling, Allhumdulillah.

Building a business helping other Muslim women feel better about themselves - even writing this chapter - is proof of what can happen when you truly accept yourself. There was a time it was unthinkable to me and now is my reality.

Prioritising your mental health and being aware of your emotions gives you so much clarity. Your belief in yourself allows you to step up, grow, evolve and take steps out of your comfort zone, which leads to great things.

I am beyond grateful that I get to share my skills and knowledge with other women and seeing the impact it has is truly amazing.

> *"Before coaching with Anieela I felt anxious, low in confidence and had low self-worth. I've been a people-pleaser for most of my life. Other people always came first and I didn't make time for myself. I didn't make an effort with my appearance. I was taking classes twice a week but was burnt out, daydreaming and barely getting things done.*
>
> *After having coaching, I am so much more productive and I focus on myself more. I've been working on my self-care and my mindset. I am letting go of the victim mindset because I realise, I have to take responsibility. Last week I attended a wedding and had an amazing time. I feel more at peace within myself. Thank you so much Anieela. You are open-minded and easy to talk to. I felt comfortable and relaxed during our coaching sessions. I feel inspired that I can achieve my goals and live a meaningful life."*
>
> — SELINA

No matter your age or what you have been through your self-acceptance and self-worth are essential. Your mental and emotional health is essential. Start the process of healing your self-acceptance wound so you can connect the dots to see how YOU feel about yourself impacts everything you do in life, including your work and relationships.

If you would like to work with me to heal your self-acceptance wound, please reach out for my signature programme.

Heal your self-acceptance wound so you can heal from the past and find love, peace and acceptance from within.

I want to take this opportunity to thank my husband for supporting me through my personal development journey and my sons - they sparked the change that led me to live the life I have always wanted. Alhumdulillah for everything Allah has bought into my life.

ABOUT THE AUTHOR
ANIEELA ARSHAD

Anieela Arshad is a Mindset and Emotional Empowerment coach who helps Muslim women feel good about themselves so they can find love, peace, and acceptance from within.

Before starting her coaching business Anieela was a stay-at-home mum while also working in network marketing. Three years in, and after having some success with her network marketing business, a change of direction came about. While having personal coaching herself, Anieela realised that her true passion was to help Muslim women to live better lives - to heal from the past and let go of negative emotions so they can truly accept themselves and enjoy the life they are living.

Anieela enjoys sketching and painting and finding natural ways to focus on her health and fitness.

Anieela is available for 1:1 coaching.

You can reach Anieela at:

Email – anieelaarshad.coaching@gmail.com

facebook.com/anieela.arshad
instagram.com/anieela.arshad.coaching

CHAPTER 3
ASSALAMUALAIKUM, I AM HAJAR.
HAJAR ABDUL HAMID

I struggled to start my chapter. I started to write many versions, only to feel something was off. Today, though, a thought crossed my mind while I was showering.

Write your truth.

So, here it is.

ASSALAMUALAIKUM, I AM HAJAR.

The girls are at it again. My daughters, eleven-year-old Hana and seven-year-old Aisha are on their school holidays and ever since they began, I have no longer had that small piece of heaven at home. I also have a two-year-old son and a nine-month-old baby girl; the former was a mutual decision between my husband and me, the latter, an "oops-I-did-it-again" gift from Allah Subhanahu wa Ta'ala. Alhamdulillah.

Between being a wife, a mami, a personal transformational coach, an entrepreneur and a working-from-home-business-owner, my life is full. I do not have any hired help for housekeeping, so I have hired, fired and rehired myself as housekeeper, cook and family chauffeur many, many times.

Each of my babies came with their own story, at different phases in my life - and this is what my story is about. So, let me start from the beginning...

Growing up, I had always had a sense that I was different from the other kids, but no one ever taught me how to celebrate my difference and how to be appreciative of myself. What usually happened was I was alienated because I thought differently and I acted differently. I could never just fit in. As I became an adult and went into the workforce, I became more and more frustrated because it seemed like nothing I did would actually get me where I wanted to be. No one ever utilised my potential and I didn't know how to do it myself.

By societal standards, I got married quite late, at the age of 31, and Hana, my firstborn, was bestowed upon us two years later. I was working as a Project Manager then. The hours were long and I mostly ignored my emotional and mental wellness. While I loved what I was doing, I started to wonder what else could I do with the skills and knowledge that I had. My answer came one evening in 2012, in the form of a radio advertisement as I was driving, to pick up my daughter from the daycare after work. It was an advertisement for a two-day short course to become a certified Professional Learning Facilitator (PLF).

I thought to myself, "Hey, I could do this. I love sharing knowledge and I can talk. I just need to learn how to convey the message properly and in an interesting way." So, I decided there and then to sign-up and the decision paid off.

The PLF program was designed to utilise Neuro-Linguistic Programming (NLP) methodologies in presenting learnings and experiences. It blew my mind. It reignited my interest in NLP and I contemplated becoming certified in it. That two-day experience was the best training journey I'd ever had at that time. I'd previously attended an NLP course in 2007. Back then, the instructor just explained it as "how you speak to your brain". And I am paraphrasing that.

This began my journey into the training industry, first as a Learning Facilitator and then, a year later, as a Lifestyle Coach. My decision to become a coach was a conscious one. It was not a product of healing from trauma or suggested by anyone. I just knew that I want to do this and help others to discover their truth too.

While pregnant with my second daughter, Aisha, I started to get interested in natural remedies and clean lifestyles. I noticed a significant difference in myself and my family and I shared the experiences with friends and family. Consequently, I became a Young Living Essential Oils distributor while in confinement. I started earning pay-check through this and my YLEO business began to grow exponentially. Two years later, I quit my corporate job as a PMO Assistant Vice President to an infotech company because my YL commissions and fees from coaching were already replacing my salary as an AVP.

THE HIGHS AND THE LOWS

So, I began my journey as a full-time business owner and entrepreneur. The year was 2017.

I soon found out that once you jump into entrepreneurship, things can be unpredictable. Sometimes your bank account is laughing, other times the crickets started playing heart-wrenching ballad songs.

In this same year, I hit my highest point and dropped to my lowest. As a YLEO distributor, I was one of many qualifiers selected for an all-expenses paid trip to the company's Lavender farm in Salt Lake City, Utah, in the United States of America. It was so exciting and a two-week holiday was planned with two of my colleagues. We would arrive a few days early in San Francisco, then fly to Utah, and after fly to Los Angeles to spend a few days there before flying back home to Kuala Lumpur. It was the trip of my dreams, visiting landmarks that I usually only watched on the television or in movies.

The morning we were preparing to go back to Kuala Lumpur, I received a call from my husband. My beloved father had returned to his Creator.

My world turned grey. I knew that I would not be able to see him for one final time. I knew there was to be no last hug, no last kiss from me or for me. I knew that the funeral procession would already be completed by the time I arrived home. I cried silently most of the journey back. I think the huge guy sitting between my colleague and me on the flight from LA to Tokyo was feeling a little weird and uneasy. I kept sniffling, my shoulders shaking at times and my colleague trying to console me every. I looked out the window and watched the clouds, sometimes seeing one in the shape of a rabbit, sometimes in the shape of a horse. And all the while I was reading the following supplication:

> "O Allah, I am your slave, the son of your slave. My forelock is in Your Hand. Your judgment of me is inescapable. Your trial of me is just. I am invoking You by all the names that You call Yourself, that You have taught to anyone in Your creation, that You have mentioned in Your Book, or that You have kept unknown. Let the Qur'an be the delight of my heart, the light of my chest, the remover of my sadness and the pacifier of my worries."
>
> — MUSNAD AHMAD

The death of my father put me on a downward spiral. I realised what I was going through. My husband would find me crying silently in my room or while I was washing the dishes. I would smile, but the smile never reached my eyes. I would read messages from friends and family telling me I was strong while in my heart, I was holding on to the rope of Allah with all my might.

In February of the following year, Allah SWT answered my du'a and put me on a journey with the Quran. For three days every week, I attended a ta'alem Quran course that supported my recovery for the next two years.

It took so long to recover because while getting myself acquainted with the grief of losing my beloved father, life was still happening for me. A cherished friendship changed its course and the hurt was slow to go away. I lost my bullet journal, which had my notes, thoughts, plans and ideas since January 2017. And in August 2018, we uprooted and move from Kuala Lumpur to Kuching (the Borneo Island part of Malaysia) leaving behind all that I knew and loved. So, there were heartbreaks and changes that I had to get used to while still coming to terms with not being able to see my father anymore.

While packing things up for the move, I had a miscarriage.

The year 2019 saw me becoming more withdrawn, looking inside to be stronger and better. Recognising the signs of depression, I kept my mind busy, taking a day at a time. Allah gifted me with an umrah trip with my mother, aunties and uncles. I made lots of du'a; for myself, my physical, emotional and mental wellness, for my deen, for my business, for my husband and children, for my mother, my siblings, family and friends. And for a son.

A week after coming back from umrah, I had my another miscarriage. I didn't even know I was pregnant. It seemed like I was experiencing loss after loss. Nothing seemed to go my way. What was it that Allah wanted me to learn? What was it that Allah wanted me to understand?

Fast forward to early 2020, while my husband was getting his cataract surgery, I went to see the ob-gyn and she confirmed that I was two months pregnant. We were cautiously excited. We found out a few months later that we would be welcoming a son. Allah SWT answered my prayer!

THEN CAME THE PANDEMIC!

And then, the world became quiet. Everyone was immobilised. I skipped some of my monthly appointments because it was safer to be at home. We were advised to avoid the hospital unless it was an emergency. While everyone was only starting to get used to being isolated - no face-to-face meetings, no gatherings, no outings - it really felt like just any other day for me. Since our move to Kuching, I stayed at home most of the time anyway, only going out for groceries or during the weekend with my husband and my girls, which included walking around the mall and eating out. I was already doing meetings and attending classes via Zoom. The pandemic did not affect me the way it did others.

Then it hit me. Allah had prepared me much earlier. He has prepped me the year before, starting with the move to Kuching. He had limited my movement and decreased my circle of contacts to that of family members and people who were important to my studies, business and personal development.

As Allah willed it, I was capitalising on my strength - being productive at times of immobility. When I looked back at my previous years, the times that I was achieving something or being productive was when I was pregnant. I passed my Project Management Professional certification while being seven months pregnant with my first child, embarked on my MBA journey when she was one year old and started my Quranic studies when I was pregnant with my second child.

2020 saw me marching forward. We welcomed our son on Malaysia's 63rd Independence Day celebration. My mother just travelled from Kuala Lumpur to Kuching three days before, planning to be with me during my confinement period, and go back after two months. Allah SWT had a different plan for us.

The second wave of the pandemic hit us about two weeks later and travelling across states was stopped again, so, my mother was stranded in Kuching for the next year. Juggling two school-going kids with a new baby, plus looking after the affairs of my elderly mother while still maintaining my own mental and emotional resilience was not an easy feat. Alhamdulillah, I made it through.

I attended Tony Robbins's "Unleash The Power Within" program online in November and Sheikh Muhammad AlShareef (Rahimullah) "DiscoverU Visionaire2030" in December. The latter jumpstarted me into action. It seemed like I found new breath and a new voice for myself.

I started making plans, putting thoughts on paper and bouncing ideas with my friends who were also collaborative partners. For the first time since that November morning in Los Angeles in 2017, I felt ready to take my place in the world. I was ready to elevate.

I GOT ANOTHER SURPRISE!

I kicked off 2021 in high gear, fully optimistic that my time to shine had come. I would be able to stand tall alongside my peers who were now becoming household names. I was happy watching their success and felt inspired to achieve mine.

I saw in my mind's eyes what it would look like. I would be working and collaborating a lot in 2021 and 2022, travelling to run programs and inspiring more people to adopt a healthy lifestyle through the usage of essential oils and essential oil-based products.

Then, we found out that we are pregnant again. We were grateful and surprised. In fact, while feeling happy and excited, my mind started to think about all my plans and ideas that now could not happen the way I planned. And it struck me, I would have to care for two babies! How was I supposed to make this work? Having to attend to one baby and working at the same time is hard enough, how was I ever going to do it with two?

I cried when I prayed. I cried while making du'a. I said to Allah, "Ya Allah... You know I have plans. You know I want to do a lot of things. I do not know how am I going to be able to do it now. Ya Allah... You know what I do not know. So, I am trusting in Your Plan. I submit to Your Timeline. Ya Allah... steer me to what is good for me, what would support my dreams and that is in line with Your Plan for me. I do not know what Your Plan is for me, but I am not going to go against it. I accept this gift you have given me Ya Allah. I ask you for Your Strength and Wisdom in bringing up four kids - something that was never in my plan."

In one of those quiet moments, I reflected, I had two miscarriages in the span of two years. And Allah SWT gifted me with two healthy babies. For all I know, both of them were my answered prayers; not just my son.

MY COACHING JOURNEY IS POLISHED

So, 2021 and 2022, instead of being the years I worked actively in the field, I was given the bandwidth to expand my skillsets and add new tools to my coaching toolbox. In these two years, I was trained in brain psychology and added one coaching methodology.

The time that I had also brought me to so many people that inspired me, and from there, those who would then help me craft better offerings for my clients and coachees. I started to become very clear about the people I want to associate myself with and those that I want to assist.

Throughout the years, one element remained constant in my own reflections and my work with my clients - everything happens for a reason, and Allah SWT wanted us to go through what we went through, be it happiness or sadness, gain or pain, so that we can be the person that we are today.

I always come back to this Hadith whenever I am self-coaching or coaching others:

> *"Strange are the ways of a believer for there is good in every affair of his and this is not the case with anyone else except in the case of a believer for if he has an occasion to feel delight, he thanks (God), thus there is a good for him in it, and if he gets into trouble and shows resignation (and endures it patiently), there is a good for him in it."*
>
> — SAHIH MUSLIM

This Hadith never failed to lift my spirits and give a reminder to be grateful always. At the end of the day, whatever happens, is for the best.

Today, I focus on assisting my clients to gain clarity on their purpose and passions. From there, I assist them in crafting their growth journey towards their goals. I mainly work 1:1 with women; I also do group coaching and facilitate project management learning programs for corporate clients.

RECOGNISING THE PASSION WITHIN

One of my major weaknesses is being too hard on myself. I overlooked saying words of appreciation to myself. I do this because part of me is thinking, I should only thank Allah because it is because of Him that I am breathing, it is due to His Will that I was able to do things that I wanted to. I am okay with thanking other people for help and assistance, but I feel weird being appreciative to myself.

No one can make us feel good about ourselves except ourselves. I learned this through failed relationships, broken friendships, and disappointment of expectations. Only I can make myself feel good, by recognising the abilities and resources that Allah has given me.

We are usually most critical of ourselves. If I ask you now to list all your shortcomings and weaknesses, I can assure you, you will be writing an essay. Instead, I am going to ask you to list all your strengths - your skills, your abilities and the resources that you have. Just list ten as a start. If you can finish that list in under two minutes, add another ten. Again, if you finished that in under five minutes, add another ten.

This is a simple test to see whether you are highly critical of yourself or have spent time recognising your own worth.

> *"Actions are according to intentions, and everyone will get what was intended."*
>
> — HADITH NAWAWI

What made you purchase this book? What made you read it, chapter by chapter? What is it that you are looking for? What do you want from the book? What do you want from your life? Where do you see yourself a year from now, a year after completing this book? What makes you wake up in the morning, ready for the day? What makes you do the things that you do?

Intentions are powerful. To find that fire within you, you have to answer these questions. So go ahead, pause your readings here and just write down the answers to these questions.

Now look back at the list that you made earlier. What is missing from the list that should be there to help you to realise your intentions? What needs to be on the list that can make your dreams come true? Did you write "Allah is my strength"? And if you did, was it your number one? Go ahead and do that now. If you did already write Allah as your number one strength, praise Allah for this awareness! Alhamdulillah.

Being able to identify and give voice to our strengths and resources is a very important step towards recognising our passion within.

Growing up, I struggled to fit in. I now realised that I need to dig within myself, accept my values and be confident in my own skin. When this happens, I see where I fit and which companies I should be with.

"IT IS ALL IN YOUR MIND"

My father, may Allah forgive and raise him, used to say this phrase to me, "It is all in your mind". I did not realise it then, but Abah (means father) was teaching me mental resiliency. He was teaching me, in not so many words, how to manage my feelings by overcoming the runaway thoughts. He was teaching me self-control and persistence.

Abah also taught me to be true to my values and to hold on to my principles. He always stressed the importance of putting the family first over friends, and doing what was needed instead of following what I wanted. He taught me to prioritise the things that I wanted and focus on the most important one.

I am of the opinion that because of this, without me realising it, I was able to overcome many challenges in my life - being the weird one amongst my peers, being bullied by my senior in boarding school, being away from the family, grieving the loss of my first pet, going through relationship breakups, facing my father's death, overcoming my pregnancy losses, dealing with failure in attaining my goals or getting my dream job, and so on.

My mother always reminded my brothers and me (I am the eldest of four siblings by the way) that Abah always had our best interests in mind. His way may be similar to the phrase "my way or the highway", but in reality, you would never get the "highway" option. Abah saw things in black and white, and there was no point spending time on the grey area. He taught us to be true to ourselves and not waver when pressured by peers.

Obviously, I was not always successful in being strong with my values and principles. I was on a learning curve and maturity often comes through falling down and making mistakes. Now, as a parent myself, reflecting on my own life events, I realise that I can never protect my children from every fall, every mistake and every heartbreak. What I can do is just to prepare them with mental resilience, emotional agility and the ability to bounce back from those events.

Abah was more focused on mental strength because he himself applied it in his life. He lived with a heart condition for more than 30 years by using his mind to overcome the occasional pain. He had the option to go through surgery but he chose not to. However, as he started to cross the sixty-year-old mark, he mentioned once that he was better at it when he was younger. With a smile of acceptance, he said it is getting tougher to tell himself that the pain is only in his mind.

From Abah's life experiences, I also learnt the power of choice. At every turn that requires a decision, we always have choices. We choose what is best for us at that point in time based on what we know about ourselves and what is available to use.

Another reminder from Abah that I recall about making choices is, "When you pick up a stick, you pick up both sides. When you make a choice or decision, you get both the good and the bad results from that decision." Once we have made the choice, we live with it until the next turn comes and we can weigh our choices again.

These two basic rules or reminders from Abah, coupled with the emotional resilience techniques that I picked up as I started my own healing journey, have truly helped me in my personal life and business. I also have to say that all these techniques must be grounded in Islamic principles for them to really work flawlessly. I have found that bringing the remembrance of Allah Subhanahu wa Ta'ala in my healing process, and in every aspect of my life, really put the "ummph!" into being strong and staying on the course.

MY LIFE TODAY

Today, I still go through ups and downs. My emotions have their moments too. Through practice and remembrance, I am able to switch my emotional states quicker and better.

It's like this - I ask myself, "How long do you want to feel this anger? I know this situation hurts you, so how long do you need to sit with it to get clarity and move forward?"

Moving forward does not mean you refuse to feel or acknowledge the feelings. Moving forward can only happen after you have taken the time to sit with the feeling that you feel, make sense of the situation that caused you to feel the feeling, take the learnings from the experience and say to yourself, "I am grateful that I learned these things from this experience and I feel this feeling because of this experience. Now this feeling has run its course, it has done its job, and I can move forward by letting it flow away."

It is like making peace within myself and understanding that I might feel this way again in different situations at different points in my life and learn something new. It is understanding that the feelings need to be appropriately felt for me to process the experience fully. It is also a reminder to me that I am human and I am alive, which means I can choose to learn from the experience, feel better and go towards other experiences. It means that I have control of my thoughts and my feelings and, as such, I can decide how long I want to be in that processing state.

The one important thing that I have to remember is that I will have to reach the end of the processing state sooner or later. I must move on from this emotional state to a new one which will serve me better.

Today, I also help others to use these steps to process their experiences. I have worked with women who needed to process anger, who felt confused, those who were betrayed or cheated, and those who are just finding their way in this life. There are women who wanted to understand their purpose and role in this life.

I once coached a business owner who had a communication issue with her partner, who was also her sister. The line between personal and professional life can be blurred in situations like this. Almost always, the parties involved will need to have a session of crucial conversation. Through the coaching session, my client unpacked her feelings and her real motivation. By the end of the fifty minutes telephone call, strong emotions have been diffused, replaced with a higher sense of being, coming from the place of understanding. She managed to come up with the best way to communicate her needs in achieving her professional goals while preserving the sisterhood bond.

Can all emotional issues and traumatic experiences be solved in one phone conversation? Not necessarily. It all depends on your history. When you have kept the emotions for so long, it is like peeling the skin of an onion. Sometimes we may be able to peel two or three layers in a day, other times, it may take more than a session to just peel one layer.

As an example, another client signed up for a six-month coaching program for leadership development and business growth. In the middle of it, an emotional event caused years of unresolved issues to come out. Through coaching conversation, it was clear that unless she resolved her past experiences fully and came to terms with her feelings, she would not be fully present and perform at her best. The coaching direction changed for her to start healing from within.

MY INVITATION TO YOU

I have told you my story. I have shared with you my approach to facing difficulties. And I have applied the same principle in assisting my clients. I now invite you to adopt the same techniques whenever you are in a difficult situation. Sometimes you can do this on your own, other times, you may need assistance with it. You may need a coach.

Start by asking yourself your true intention. What is that you want? What would you like to see happen as the outcome of the process?

Then start looking at what is available within your control, what resources you can use to help you move forward. Name the feeling that you are feeling and try to make sense of it. Ask yourself, what makes you feel this feeling? Is it really the first feeling that you feel when the event happened? Or is it the feeling that comes after you tried to understand the situation?

Next, start looking at options. What can you do knowing now the reason you are in that state? What is the next emotion that you need to feel to move on or to change your state? How long are you going to allow yourself to be in this state?

Finally, take action. When do you want to feel better? Decide. Now.

About the Author
HAJAR ABDUL HAMID

Hajar Abdul Hamid is a clarity and growth coach based in the beautiful city of Kuching, Sarawak, where she lives with her amazing husband and four wonderful children. Originally from the bustling city of Kuala Lumpur, Hajar earned her degree in Information Technology from UKM Bangi and later her MBA from East London University. She spent over 15 years as a dedicated project manager before following her passion and becoming a coach.

Hajar is a warm and caring person who loves helping women achieve their dreams and live fulfilling lives. As a clarity and growth coach, she's passionate about empowering women to discover and embrace their unique potential. Her clients describe her as a knowledgeable and compassionate coach who truly cares about their success.

In her free time, Hajar loves to read and relax with her family. She's also a big believer in living a healthy, natural lifestyle and advocates for it through her coaching practice. Hajar enjoys the beauty and tranquillity of the ocean and believes she can be a great gardener. She's also currently attending a Quran Arabic course to deepen her connection with her faith and become a better person every day.

Hajar is also an ambitious entrepreneur, running her own home-based business as a network marketer. She's a true inspiration to women who want to have it all, and her energy and enthusiasm are infectious.

Connect with Hajar here:

shajar.ahamid@gmail.com

www.hajarhamid.com

CHAPTER 4
THE LIGHT AT THE END OF THE LONGEST TUNNEL
MAHIRA HASANOVIC

I was standing in the shallow end of the pool, holding my youngest daughter in my arms. I felt the tension in my cheeks from holding a smile for too long. I must have looked like I was a million miles away, but it felt like only a few seconds had passed before I was startled back to reality. "What are you thinking about?" my mother's voice said. I slowly turned my body towards her before beginning to speak. "You know, mum, this is it. This is life," I began, "Right here, mum… It isn't in some big events we so often seem to wait for, it's right here in these imperfect, joyous moments". The look on her face gave me no information as to what she thought. Was she happy for me or confused by me? It didn't matter because in this moment, I saw the incredible journey I had made and I was happy. I was happy that after what almost felt like a decade of some of the most difficult times of my life, some of my greatest failures, I had arrived at such profound internal peace.

A joyous peace. I felt positive about the future and about my place in the world. My love for my religion had grown enormously and I had such a positive view of God. I felt lucky!

This may not have made sense to anyone given that I was a single mother of soon-to-be three children, but I felt so lucky to have been dealt the cards that I was. I saw the reason in every hand, I saw the bigger picture and I was honoured. I needn't anyone to hand me their approval. If God was pleased with me, I was going to continue to smile until my face hurt. And I did... often.

A long time ago, I too fell for the lie that what I needed was a perfect life to be happy. I had to be perfect, and it had to be perfect. I had to be the perfect Muslim woman, have the perfect husband, the perfect kids and absolutely everything had to look exactly how the community dictated. I scoff and giggle at this now but then these were my subconscious beliefs that kept me frozen and in a state of shame because I felt like I was constantly failing. The pressure I was putting on myself was not motivating me but instead actually keeping me from being happy and fuelling my negative self-talk.

To my younger self and to anyone who finds themselves in that state, a state where self-awareness seems to fuel self-critique I would say: go easy. You haven't done anything close to being deserving of such constant berating. You need not be ashamed of making the best choices with what you knew at the time. You need not care for the opinions of people who won't be helping you put your children to bed at night, paying your bills or sharing any difficult moments with you. They don't think about you as much as you worry they do, believe me. Don't live for people. If it's ok with God then it really is ok. You need no one else's permission to choose what is best for you.

In my 20s, the outside world seemed to perceive me as someone very confident and as someone who knew exactly what she wanted. While I recognise that I have always had a natural strength passed down from the women in my family, rather than confident I was a person who was very unsure of herself. Every time I would grasp at what seemed to be "it" and get a handle on some sort of direction, it would just as quickly slip away: many projects were started and unfinished, many books bought and unread, many good habits picked up and dropped soon after. I felt sort of frantic internally, wanting so much to solve the puzzle so I could just be on track. But all that pushing did nothing but create more resistance and keep me frozen. It felt like every time I would take one step forward, I would also take one back. I kept going down that path, researching *what was wrong with me* and how I was going to fix myself, spending hours and hours taking in information via Instagram, YouTube and Facebook. At the time, I thought would bring me the answers I needed but instead I was left more exhausted and more stuck. This was part of my pattern, always looking externally for validation and solutions. It was a reflection of how disconnected I was from myself and how little trust I had in my own internal guidance system.

I was haunted by my past mistakes, by failed relationships and business ideas that never amounted to much. I remember being told that I was the first person in my family to go through a divorce (little did they know, I was going to be the first to do many things) and even being pushed away by certain people I held close because I didn't listen to their advice to "stay and be patient" when faced with abuse. At the time, this filled me with shame. I kept thinking this was a personal shortcoming and even that it made God unhappy with me. I found myself, at the age of 26, divorced and a single parent.

It was a sobering time, but not sobering enough. I was about to learn that God has a way of turning up the heat on anything we choose to ignore in life. In my mind, I was doing things differently now and I was not going to follow the same patterns of self-abandonment to be in a relationship. Surely this would lead me to a successful marriage in the future. What I didn't understand was that even with so much new knowledge and progress, my subconscious mind was actually running the show and so much unresolved childhood trauma was going to lead me into similar patterns.

I was just four years old when we had to flee our city because it was under siege. The Serbian forces had occupied the city and we had no choice but to leave everything behind. The adults carried what they could fit onto their backs and into their hands for the trip on foot. My father knew he had no chance of getting out with us as they were going to capture the men. He attempted to escape through a forest with his brother and other men. The group split in two and he was separated at a certain point from his brother. His brother made it out. We never saw my father again.

I only have flashes of what took place - trucks, men taking my elderly grandfather away, a boy with a bleeding head, a metal milk flask being thrown to the side of the dirt road, the hard candy I found in the food pallets thrown from helicopters. I also remember leaving food packets for my dad for when he returned. I was dearly attached to him, yet I never remember being sad in those early days. My mother sheltered my three siblings and me from all harm and none of us but my 12-year-old sister understood that we were in any danger at all. She did that for years to come and in her words, she was "our mother and father". She made sure we were not cold or hungry. I never even saw her cry.

Only when I got older did I understand the significance of what took place. It was always interesting to me that the older I got, the more I felt the void and consequence of my father's death.

I grew up in a single-parent home. First in Bosnia, then in Australia from the age of 10. We moved about seven times before my 18th birthday, but I am grateful that each time it was to a better place. My mother spent much of her time fending for us. I remember asking her if she would ever be one of those mums who cooked for us while we sat waiting for breakfast at the kitchen counter in the morning, but she didn't have that luxury at the time.

I grew into a young adult who had little to no autonomy. On the outside, I always appeared to "have it together" but internally I had no boundaries and no self-trust. I felt quite empty and invisible, I was plagued by guilt at the thought of putting myself first, and above all, I felt like a scared child, afraid of really asserting myself in the world. I became the carer, the fixer and the saviour, and this was most amplified in my romantic relationships. The unresolved trauma drew me towards abusive or exploitative relationships. After each relationship ended, I always thought that the next time would be perfect, but I now know that what we intend does not happen unless we deal with the root cause of the issues… and I hadn't done that. I could not attract into my life what was not present inside of me, no matter how strongly I intended it. My reality was a mirror to the healing that was not done. Every few weeks, I felt like my mind and body went into shutdown mode. During those periods, I found it difficult to function and did the bare minimum. I couldn't grasp any meaning or motivation. It made me feel like an awful Muslim and an awful mother. Sometimes it seemed to come out of nowhere and I was at its mercy. The help I had sought out kept me in a state of coping but never truly healing. This went on for so many years that I wondered if I was ever going to become the woman I dreamed of being - Vibrant and successful and in love with life and God, the woman I knew I had the potential to be but back then, in my mind, I had failed.

This constant repetition of negative behavioural patterns perhaps took the biggest toll on my mental health. I felt like I was swimming in the middle of the ocean and as soon as I would get to the surface and take a breath, I was met with another crushing wave that pushed me back under, deeper this time.

That is what depression felt like for me, drowning and not being heard or seen. It was interesting to be so self-aware and yet feel so helpless in moving forward. When I began to understand that I was playing out ingrained programming from my childhood, things got worse before they got better.

I started my second marriage on a high before I noticed that my choices were still leading me to relive the most painful patterns of my early years - the pattern of not feeling chosen and prioritised and even feeling invisible. As expected, things started to fall apart and the shame and isolation that came this time were more intense than before. "What in the world is wrong with me?", "I'm never going to get it right", "What will people say?" "Again!"

This is when I knew I had to seek effective help from someone who aligned with my religion and my values. I simply couldn't imagine taking another step in the same direction. I was entirely desperate for change and out of that state, real change happened. God brought me to a place where I couldn't imagine living like this for another year, or even another month, to move me to take a different path. As strong as that voice for change became during that time, real change is never linear and there were other voices present too "Maybe this is just life, maybe I'm asking too much, maybe it really doesn't get better than this". This feeling was, at times, reinforced by what I saw around me - people who went along with the status quo and held it up even, whose light dimmed with each passing year and who seemed to live for the material pleasures of life. I thank God that the internal need for change won in the end. It was a spark that wouldn't die. A deep knowing and yearning for something better, something healthier. This.is.not.it! I would tell myself. I couldn't accept that life had to be this hard and painful... and dull. After all, God was limitless so who was I to limit Him?

I can sometimes pick up on people's confusion as to why I am so positive. Why am I not drained? Why am I not negative and miserable? Don't I feel hard done by? I should be all of those things, right? Yet I'm not. How is that possible?

It's simple really, I've done and continue to do the work - the real, from the roots up, work.

Once I began working with my coach and addressing a lifetime of trapped emotions and trauma, that's when the real, long-lasting mental shifts started for me. Simultaneously, I was studying to become a coach myself and received my certifications in multiple therapy modes.

Rather than taking you through the step-by-step process, I will explain what happened internally for me to be able to take on such a new mindset and begin thriving rather than surviving.

Imagine you work in an office and along the wall exists an enormous sliding filing system. In it is every piece of paper the business has ever produced and more. You've only added files into it, never removed them, pulling out one or two occasionally to refer to them before putting them back. You talk for years about this cabinet and how it's not serving you properly and in fact, it's creating issues for you in your place of business, yet you only ever dust the outside of it and let it continue to sit with all its contents. You ask the cleaner to help but she dusts the shelves and goes on her way. Every time you look at it, it overwhelms you, so you put it off longer until one day it's so overstuffed that files begin to spill out. Not only can you not find what you need, but now, things that should be kept private are scattered on the floor. There is no choice left but to do something about this. You don't know where to start until a friend gives you a contact and the help they offer is exactly what you need. They come in and you are nervous, but you needn't be because, as you soon find out, they know precisely what is needed here. Finally, the files are opened. Everything that is not needed is tossed out. Some of it you realize wasn't even yours! Most of it is no longer in use. A new filing system is put into place, and it works beautifully! It's so incredibly organized it seems to gleam when you look at it. You can breathe, you feel so incredibly light. That which you avoided you now can't wait to utilise. The success of the clean-up is felt throughout the business. You can't quite believe how such a simple change has had such a profound effect and you can't help but rant to whoever will listen about the changes you've made. The only thing you now think about is why didn't you do it sooner?!

My mind was like this overstuffed filing cabinet. Talk therapy felt like dusting off the shelves which desperately needed clearing. Taking in information via social media etc. felt like I was adding more files before the others were cleared out and organised.

I had held onto pain and fear that were not even mine but passed onto me. This was followed by a lifetime of accumulated negative emotions and beliefs that were keeping me frozen or in fight or flight mode. Intuitively, I knew that dealing with the root causes of the issues would create the change needed and my answers lay with the subconscious. Healing at the subconscious level was going to create change the change I was yearning for.

As touched upon previously, I had attended talk therapy for quite a few years before finding out about Neuro Linguistic Programming and Timeline Therapy. Not only did I need this, but I felt "everyone needed this". I felt like I had found the answer to so much of my frustration.

Clearing negative emotions using timeline therapy felt like a new lease on life… but it was just the beginning.

Slowly, I phased out interactions with people whose presence was detrimental to me and I learned to gracefully set boundaries with others. I became a watcher of my inner voice and emotions instead of being overwhelmed by them. What I have come to understand is that the negative voices one may play in their mind is not their voice at all. It is the accumulation of others' critiques from when we were little. It is our own fear disguised as that voice. Fear thinks it's helping us by keeping us safe. It believes that to be its job, and it is, but to move forward we must ask fear to sit this one out. Imagine that negative self-talk as a person in the corner of the room, sitting with their head down and afraid. What would you feel towards them? Most likely, rather than thinking them to be right, you would feel sympathy towards them - maybe you'd even offer them comfort. You are the observer in that room and the one who gets to make the decisions. Once I fully internalised this, I stopped giving negative self-talk any power and so the volume was turned down almost to mute.

Permission. This was a big one. I gave myself permission to decide for myself what was the best direction to take. It's incredible how often we, as women, feel like we need the approval or permission of others to do the things that we intuitively know are right. Now that I was connected to my inner guidance system, I felt more confident than ever that I was headed in the right direction. I understood that I didn't need to have the next ten, or even five years of my life figured out, I just needed to know the next step. Intuition is a great consultant and it's free! Use it. Use it to figure out the next step and the road will become more and more clear. And when redirected, don't be afraid to change course.

Something I have not heard discussed very often in mainstream healing circles is the need to heal our relationship regarding how we view our religion and how we view God. This step, in my opinion, is critical and without it, all the other work we do will be incomplete. There is one question that really shook me awake and it was "Whose voice have you assigned to God?"

I understand that is a strange and maybe even shocking question for someone to read but if answered honestly, it will lead you to a greater understanding of how we limit God in our minds, though He, of course, is limitless and in no way diminished by our restricted way of thinking. For me, I quickly realised that the punishing, displeased, harsh voice I assigned to God was the voice of critical Islamic teachers and other men in my past and present. It was then that I decided to look for scholars that uplifted and inspired me, rather than kept me frozen and shame-filled. In my heart, I knew that if my understanding of religion changed in a way that increased my practice of said religion, then it was the correct path to take. That is how I navigated the internal question of "how do you know this is right?", I sought out others who thought like me and began to fall in love again with my religion just like I knew I could. With this, my gratitude and happiness increased. I felt like God was on my side and I was going to improve slowly and steadily in my worship out of love and devotion. This new mindset also allowed me to smile at life's circumstances knowing all my trials were good for me. Everything had happened with good reason, and I could turn my pain into absolute treasure if I so wanted.

There are times when it still feels something like a dream to finally have the mindset of the woman I always wanted to be, to be working with other women and helping them get there also... Actually, no, this feels even better than I had dreamed.

Healing isn't having a blissful life with no trials or difficulties. I experience life's challenges just like everyone, but I do so without overwhelm. Because I have grown as a person, they seem so much smaller, less significant and always solvable. My decision-making is in tune with my inner self so my reality looks more and more like a life that is in alignment with who I am - a life that I am pleased to wake up for. My days are filled with little moments of joy and even on the days I feel like I may have failed to do all I wanted, I don't feel any less driven to keep going. My understanding of life, process and patience is so much greater and brings me such peace. It is my wish to teach this to as many women as possible.

I once read that bravery is an island in an ocean of fear. Turning your life around in such a dramatic way requires just that. A lot of us like to say that we wish to change but what if I said to you "ok, let's do that right now"? What would be the response inside your body to that? Would it be to freeze? Would your breath stop for a minute? Or would it be a full-body yes? All of those responses are normal and ok and you are still able to make the decision to act while being afraid. What you must never do is become complacent and stagnant, give up on progress or even worse, put up with toxic situations. It will always come back to bite you in the long term.

I want you to answer the following questions with as much honesty as possible:

If you stayed living exactly as you are right now for the rest of your life and you came to the moment of your death, would you regret what your life amounted to?

If you stayed exactly as you are and your children were grown and had moved on and you looked around at what remained, would you be satisfied?

If your body could no longer take how much you had repressed and you lay sick in a hospital bed, would it have been worth it?

Can you keep doing this for another five years?
If you knew God would be pleased with you nonetheless, what would you change about your life today?

I know that those are heavy questions. In times of stuckness and numbness, we sometimes need sobering questions that hit just the right nerve to bring us back to reality about what is at stake here. It's our entire life and even the lives of others that are at play. Healing does not happen in a bubble. It is like a ripple in a pond of water, it travels out and is felt across the whole surface. That is something you are capable of effecting.

It's time for real change. Bring your fear if you need to, but bring your resolution also. If I was able to overcome the immense trauma holding me back, you most certainly can, and if you say you will, I believe you will. This work is for the brave and just by picking up this book to read, I know you are one of them.

ABOUT THE AUTHOR
MAHIRA HASANOVIC

Mahira Hasanovic was born in Bosnia & Herzegovina and now resides in South Australia with her three children. Her personal challenges have led her to pursue a career in helping others like herself overcome their trauma and heal. After pursuing extensive qualifications, she now practices as a coach to Muslim women. It is her desire to reach as many women as possible with her message of hope regardless of their past.

You can connect with Mahira here:

mahira.hasanovic@gmail.com

CHAPTER 5
WELCOME HOME! THE HOME I'VE BEEN SEARCHING FOR HAS ALWAYS BEEN WITHIN ME

MAZADA AHMED, SELF-LOVE QUEEN, UNITED KINGDOM

> "Everything I need is within me!"
>
> — LOUISE HAY

You are beginning to understand, aren't you? You're beginning to realise that the whole world is inside you: in your perspectives and in your heart, and to be able to find peace, you must be at peace with yourself first; and to truly enjoy life, you must enjoy who you are. Once you learn how to master this, you will be protected from everything that makes you feel like you cannot go on. With this gift of recognising yourself, even when you are alone, you will never be lonely. As I pondered on these deep epiphanies, my thoughts flashed back to my traumatic past.

For most of my life, I've been a positive person. My family and friends nicknamed me 'positive queen' My colleagues would describe me as a confident and bold woman.

It was in the year 2011 that my life turned upside down. I had an arranged marriage to a person I thought was perfect for me. Unfortunately, the marriage lasted only a few months during which time, I was made to feel like I was not worthy of living in this world. I ended up completely shattered and my confidence was destroyed.

I was a newly-wedded bride going to live with her in-laws. I was jubilant and nervous at the same time at the thought of entering a new household of strangers. A few weeks into the marriage, my nightmares came to life. My ex-husband neither supported me financially nor emotionally. I could not connect with my him. We were like two different poles that had nothing in common to connect and bond us. He never seemed to understand me at all and seemed to find fault in everything I did. His was an isolated family while mine was a big, close-knit loving family where members look out for each other and I often felt I had to choose between my husband and my family.

As I was a people-pleaser, I was quick to believe the gaslighting and undermining and I blamed myself for things going wrong in my match-made marriage. Soon, I lost my identity as a loving, bubbly girl and became someone who could not voice out her feelings. I fell into the depths of anxiety. As I was the eldest girl in my family, I did not want to immediately file for divorce, thinking that if I did, I would be setting a bad example to my younger sisters, but eventually, there came a trigger point where I just had to pack my bags. I was separated from my ex-husband for months. It was very difficult to get a divorce as he moved house and was unreachable. I was so hopeless. Then, I turned to Allah. I found peace in praying and asking Allah to guide me.

After this much-needed space and separation, I was finally granted a divorce. Although freedom was obtained through the divorce, I was a lost girl and I became numb to my surroundings and feelings. I hid myself away under the pretext of longer working hours to avoid thinking of my divorce trauma. I laughed and smiled at my workplace and in front of my parents - I was sweeping the dirt under the carpet and acting as if I was feeling ok. Although I was numbing myself, I leaned more and more on my Islamic faith for divine guidance. And, sure enough, guidance did come in the guise of embracing healing modalities and self-love.

I used the following supplication prior to receiving this divine guidance:

"Rabbi Inni lima anzalta ilayya min khayrin faqeer.":

— QURAN 28:24 (MEANING: MY LORD, I AM IN TRULY GREAT NEED OF ANY GOOD THAT YOU MIGHT SEND DOWN TO ME.)

In 2014, I began my self-development journey and have since been obsessed with learning and growing in all areas of my life. I've invested heavily in my personal growth, taken many coaching programs, hired a 1:1 coach, joined group coaching sessions and also attended many workshops.

In 2016, I had a stint working in the United Arab Emirates. Soon, my lifestyle started changing as I was exposed to a new work environment and new colleagues. I've been blessed to have learned and achieved a lot in my life.

In 2019, I had the opportunity to attend the famed Lisa Nichols's live workshop, **'The Art & Science of Impact Speaking'**. On the last day, we worked on the concept of 'Forgiveness'. During the course, I was asked to write about a person I would love to forgive in my life. I thought I had forgotten my ex-husband, but when I thought of forgiving him for all the pain and hurt I felt because of him, tears were streaming down my cheeks. I could not do it. I could not forgive the person who turned my life upside down. I could not forgive him... and I could not forgive myself. That's when I realised that I have not grieved my loss in the divorce properly and had not forgiven myself or my ex-husband fully.

While I was in the UAE, I was encouraged by my mum to meet potential new partners and move forward with my life, but I could not connect with the people I met. They were emotionally unavailable. I was quite frustrated as I was ready to settle down. Why couldn't I find a decent man to settle down with?

My mother wanted me to move back to London and find myself a husband and I decided to move back to London in July 2019. It was my sister's engagement and I was busy helping her with that. Even though I wasn't actively searching, deep down, I was hoping to meet someone and settle down.

I was tired of meeting emotionally unavailable men. I exhausted myself. I decided to take a break from searching. I needed to dive deep to find out why I was meeting emotionally unavailable potentials.

It was the end of November 2019 and I was scrolling through Facebook. I came across a poster by Aafia about a two-day workshop on emotional and energy healing. I was so desperate to find out why I couldn't find a decent person to settle down with, I decided to attend the workshop. At that workshop, I finally forgave and released my ex-husband from my heart and mind.

I made a decision to take one hundred per cent accountability for myself and start my healing journey. I wanted to find myself and rebloom into the beautiful flower I have always been so, I checked myself into different healing modalities to release my trauma and pain in the marriage. Emotional Freedom Technique (EFT) and Rapid Transformational Therapy (RTT) came to my rescue to fully heal myself. I also picked up on emotional healing and energy to keep my emotions in check and increase my self-love and self-worth. I was once again introduced to the concept of forgiveness in these healing modalities. I continued to do the inner child healing work consistently. I realised that forgiveness is for me to accept myself for who I am and love myself fully despite my mistakes and that I practice forgiveness for myself and not for the other person who has wounded me in my life. That feeling was so liberating.

I had to go deeper within and I understand myself through journaling and meditation. I used Ho'oponopono and hypnosis.

I did everything I could to change my belief and self-concept. The journey wasn't easy. I cried and often felt like giving up.

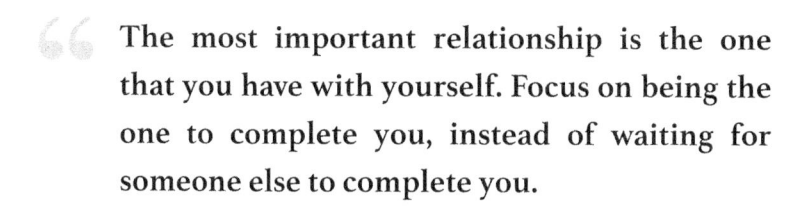

> **The most important relationship is the one that you have with yourself. Focus on being the one to complete you, instead of waiting for someone else to complete you.**

This is something that I've learnt over the years. I always thought that I needed someone else to complete me and make me feel whole. I used to tell people I want someone to complete me.That's when I didn't know anything about self-love or self-development. I don't know where I picked it up but I believe it was from society.

Don't get me wrong, I love being in love, BUT I don't seek it out in order to make me feel complete. I'm wholesome and complete within myself.

Throughout my healing and self-love journey, I've realised it's my responsibility to feel complete. I complete myself as a person. I'm not a half. I'm a whole person. I stand strong with myself.

You are the person that you spend the most time with. You are the one that understands you the most. Therefore, it's so important to treat yourself with the love and kindness that you freely give to others.

It's important to build a healthy and strong relationship with yourself because, when you do meet someone, they will compliment your vibe instead of completing it.

You won't NEED them to want or complete you but you'll WANT them, which is so better in my eyes.

The Almighty Allah was showing that I am whole and enough as a person and I have found the HOME that I was searching for, deep in my soul all along. I've embodied self-love.

As a self-love Queen, I now see my truth. I've built a resilient mindset. I'm emotionally strong enough to handle any situation. My empowerment, to put it in a nutshell, lies in discernment and wisdom. I own my imperfections as they make me human and I know that I'm always loved and good enough.

With this newfound enthusiasm, and filled with so much self-love, women now flock to hear my survival story to spearhead their own self-love stories. I have these three success actions for women on the path of self-love and self-empowerment.

Three Success Actions:

1. Don't rely on a man to complete you! You are whole and worthy!
2. Take 100% responsibility for your life.
3. Dust your Queen voice and begin to speak loud and clear.

> "Remember, you have been criticizing yourself for years and it hasn't worked.
>
> Try to approve yourself and see what happens!"
>
> — LOUISE HAY

Moving forward in my thirties, I have annihilated my self-loathing and come out of my darkness. I am finally HOME, which has been within me all this while. I'm now embracing my light and becoming a beacon of light for women in darkness to heal themselves through my 'Self-Love' Movement.

Self-Love is accepting yourself as you are. Embrace your flaws, your strengths and your weaknesses

When you truly love yourself, you will be confident to stand up for yourself. Self-Love will set you free.

The more you love yourself, the less you will seek validation from others.

About the Author
MAZADA AHMED

My name is Mazada, welcome to my world.

I'm a Self-Love and Mindset Coach, Philanthropist and world traveller with an obsession for mastering every area of my life, fulfilling my potential as a human being and making a difference in the lives of Muslim women.

I help single Muslim women find clarity, joy and love through healing past traumas. I help them to build a healthy relationship with themselves and show up unapologetically.

Reclaim your power back.

With love and gratitude

Mazada

CHAPTER 6
FREEDOM FROM THE SHACKLES OF SOCIETY
SALMA ZHAID

As I sit here, writing my goals, I know that I am finally on the journey of reaching the goals I set for myself years ago. Those once-anticipated calls I waited for from organisations that I felt I could assist are finally coming and the goal of becoming an active community leader and having a successful company is very much within my reach.

My dream of seeing women become confident and achieve their best selves is no longer just a certificate in a frame. My credentials mean nothing when I am not hearing or learning of a woman's ambitions being achieved thanks to our company or myself, as a coach and therapist.

I know now that being the person that I chose to become for others has led me to become the successful community leader I am today. I say with gratitude that this position I hold is not for people who just strive for money and see only their benefit in the outcome. I've learned that it is essential to prioritise teamwork as your success is due to everyone in that team.

Over the years, I have made sacrifices and shown patience, as well as a lack of perfection. I learnt over time, that being perfect was never a possibility and that getting things done should be the ultimate goal.

My coaching journey began when my marriage ended. I believed it was going to help build my confidence in relationships, but it did more than that. It has helped me build as a person, a guide, a mentor and even a leader. Once you believe in yourself, perfection doesn't exist and neither does the fear of what others will say.

Join me as I walk you through ways to freedom, from the shackles of society. It is the journey of someone who always cared about bringing herself up to standard, only to realise that sometimes, we need to be armoured through lessons and trials for times when we are no longer relying on others.

At school, I knew that I didn't fit in. I knew I felt different and wasn't able to think and act like the other girls. I loved reading, so most time would spend alone lost in a book. I always wanted more, to know more and spent time alone to ponder over my thoughts and ideas. I dreamed of being a bubbly character but was labelled as practical and boring by some of my friends and told that I didn't know how to have fun. I told myself I would have to show them I could and that I was just as fun as them. What I realise now is that their fun was different to mine. A good book and good company were, and still are, good enough for me. School was also a time of bullying for me. I regularly faced different kinds of abuse, from racial abuse to being fat-shamed. Mostly, I tried I brush it under the carpet. I didn't want to fight back as my values didn't allow it but staying quiet didn't make the bullying go away. I had to do something, that was more effective than fighting back, so I chose to believe in myself and stand my ground. I had to show that I was confident with what and who I was, even though inside I felt my insides imploding with tears. I was eventually able to ignore them and it seemed they eventually got bored and left me alone.

This was a lesson for me and it was reinforced at university where, unlike at school, I tended to stick close to a few close friends who appreciated me, rather than try to be who I wasn't. The rest would come and go.

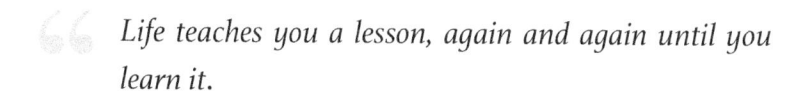

> *Life teaches you a lesson, again and again until you learn it.*

Overall though, uni was great - the friends, socialising and of course, the healthy pressure of assignments and deadlines. I enjoyed my time and learnt a lot about myself. I was a chilled individual, who had principles and values. I loved socialising but knew my limits, I believed in myself and was great at debates. I still am, if anyone wants to try me.

After university, I entered the workforce where I was made to feel that I was never good enough. I stepped up confidently though and made sure that I did my best. My goal became clear; I should work hard to step up the ladder and show those who appreciated my work that I was capable of more. I was able to adjust and realign myself to both become better and show that I wouldn't be discouraged by any negative feedback. I was able to do this in many ways and thus kept myself in check regularly, to make sure I was doing what was expected and more. When I moved onto a new role, it felt like the best decision. I did everything a manager did and made sure that I treated my team well, as I knew that the leader's attitude has an impact on the whole team, socially and mentally. I managed to keep up with the needs of the team and the company.

After 10 years of working in the same company and learning many roles and skills in nearly every department, I realised that sometimes it's OK not to have everything. I had gained as much as I could and my time there geared me up for my future role as an events manager, community worker and more.

I've always felt lucky to have a loving family. We can't choose family but although we can all be a bit nutty sometimes, we know the love will always be with us. We are always there if someone needs us - if we can't help them, we'll find someone that will. But even though I knew all this, I still had trust issues, which lead to a huge gap in my marriage. I got married, straight after my degree, hoping to carry on with my education and even spoke to my then-husband about future goals. I soon realised his ideas were very different and we were going to clash now and then. I decided I wouldn't impose too many of my values and goals on my husband, I would try to be the good wife and "compromise", as I was told we do in a marriage. In time, we had an understanding and started a family. Things did not run smoothly with my first-born, but we both did our best and although we had our ups and downs, we lived it out. We did it for our son's sake because we loved him, and slowly but surely, we started to work together, to buy a home for our family.

Our second child was born in 2012. This was a year of peaks and troughs and helped shape my future. I believed, as a strong-minded woman, I would overcome any issues that came up, but I found myself becoming weak. I was constantly hearing comments about the shape of his head. He had hydrocephalus (fluid in the brain), and had seemingly never-ending crying episodes. Every time there was a gathering, I would cringe, as I knew he would cry and my loving and doting family - who I love - would try to help but make things worse. We had tests done and were told we should be prepared, for surgery on shunts in the brain. This would drain the fluid from the brain. I did not know how it worked and wasn't prepared to find out. I blocked out a lot of what the doctors said.

Then, the opportunity of a lifetime knocked - Hajj, the pilgrimage, the trip of a lifetime. We had the resources and family were going, so we decided to book the trip. I had heard that prayers were answered in the holiest of places. I wasn't going to let this one go. My son was born in June, after an emergency C-Section and we booked Hajj (Pilgrimage to Makkah) in October. Mum's words of love and concern for her daughter still rings in my ears. I felt empowered then. I had the support I needed and knew my children would be safe without me. It felt normal because I felt I was going from one home to another.

As I saw the miracles of the two holiest cities, I saw all the male pilgrims wearing just two white sheets and the women wearing simple attire that covered them modestly. This was a wake-up call for me and a reminder that we are all equal in His eyes. We are only separated by piety and knowledge of good and this can only be shown by a person's heart and actions of good manners and patience.

I had read up on Hajj but I was completely humbled by the mercy of the Almighty. We were told that our prayers would be answered in front of the Kaaba, at the Rawdha (resting place) of our beloved Prophet (peace upon him) and mount Arafat, where we all stood and prayed for His mercy, forgiveness, and ease in affairs. I took all the opportunities and prayed sincerely for the first time in a while. I prayed for my child's well-being and the strength that I needed to bring him up in this world. I prayed every day for His mercy and forgiveness and, deep inside, my love for my Creator grew, every day, knowing that everything we have is because of Him.

Every time we are tested, it is because He loves us and wants us closer to Him. I knew all of this and knew that this was my lantern, the light I will always carry. I knew then that no matter what happened, He would be with me and that the support I needed would always be there.

On my way back from the holiest of places, all I could think of was my son and his condition. What would happen? What would the doctors have to say? Had my prayers been answered?

A few weeks of regular hospital visits led to a week where my son and I stayed and waited for his turn to be checked. The doctors ordered them to keep the baby hungry for up to six hours until his MRI, as he would need an anaesthetic. This took a lot out of me. I took every opportunity, to be back on the floor praying. I left Ismail with the nurses and when I felt I needed a spiritual connection, I would go back to the faith room to be alone and just pray for everything to become easy. I knew my son needed me. I also wanted to make sure I was doing everything I could to make all of this go away. The thought of brain surgery was not what I thought I could handle for myself and my child - at least not as I imagined the procedure.

A few days later, I recall the rush to the MRI department. The moment they gave my son the anaesthetic, he went limp in my arms and my heart skipped a beat as the emotions overtook me. As strong as I wanted to be, I was a mum and the thought of what could be was taking over my emotional strength.

The wait for news was agitating. The doctor came within a few minutes but they felt like hours. *"You can take him home,"* he said, *"we couldn't find a blockage".*

I felt a rush of gratitude, happiness, excitement and everything else all at once. So, as before, I left him with the nurse and prayed my gratitude prayer. All praise be to Him, the Almighty

This was huge, this was a miracle and I knew after that I would never lose hope again. Even today, when I look back, I relive the feelings and let them wash over me, as I pray for a brighter future for my children.

Derby 2014

In 2014, we moved to Derby, with the lessons I had learned from what I now refer to as a *previous life* and I love it here.

After all that I had seen and the way I was treated and felt, it finally felt as though I was pitching up for a life of independence and leadership. I help women and families, in my community, to grow confident and share their worries and concerns. I share my story, so they feel that they'll get through it. I have been given so many opportunities that I had only imagined a few years ago.

When my parents ask me, lovingly, to come back home, I remind them that now this is my home and I feel connected to my roles. It felt that I could do lots in the new home, that I wouldn't have been given the opportunities for back home. I wasn't well known in the wider community, and their vision was not the same as mine.

But how did I get to this place?

In 2014, I found myself always trying to please others. I offered free selling stalls at my community events to many women that asked and said were struggling. That was my way of serving the locals. I wanted to be liked as I was new to the area and no one knew me. I was in the mindset that good things will only happen when I serve the community by going the extra mile. As I carried on this way, I saw other small companies and charities become so much bigger within the community and beyond.

As I compared my organisation to others, I thought it would look good if I collaborated with other local companies, which resulted in a lack of appreciation from them and resulted in the footfall at my events becoming smaller; this was a result of my lack of focus and personal growth. I should have believed in myself to achieve the best. I had the right tools, including contacts and marketing techniques, but it just didn't feel like enough. I was good at building relationships with people and that was what had always worked for me in the past and would in the future.

I built the events business to a stage where as soon as I advertised my events, the ladies were calling, and I would usually be booked within a week. All the hard work of cold messaging around 100 people just in and around Derby had worked. It paid off to act like the manager, leader, organiser, marketer and even accountant. I fulfilled all of these roles to achieve this height.

Then, after almost three years of smooth sailing, covid hit. Lockdown meant, no contact with anyone in person, so the events had to be cancelled. I was dealing with a broken marriage and a dream that had halted. The children became very emotional and it was something that I was finding less easy to handle. By the grace of the Almighty, I was classified as a keyworker, so my children were allowed to attend their school, under very strict conditions. I still had my baby at home, which was just about manageable.

I made use of my free time - I helped oversee the local foodbank, answered crisis phone calls, delegated tasks to the team and still made time for the family. After a year of this, I received a phone call requesting help to raise money through social media and radio. Excitement hit, as another dream project unfolded.

The phone call was one sent from above, as they say.

"Salaams sister, pray you're well... we heard you do lots of work with women and have a good network. We need help to build a

girls' college in Pakistan... as you're a sister we believe your input would be most beneficial..."

At the time, I ended the conversation, with "Yes, I will, and of course, education should be for all".

The visualisation I had of a girls' college didn't come to me as expected, but it was the same concept, purpose and ambition that I had. I had planned and visualised a girls' college here in the UK. I knew there was a lot of work involved and it would take all my time, to prepare and build it. I also knew that when it *was* the right time - the plan would unfold in ways that were not imaginable at the time.

I felt honoured to be part of such an inspirational project. The history of Pakistan, going back around a century ago, was that there was no free education available to the poor. They would always lose out when it came to this opportunity. Even after achieving these opportunities, boys would get the right to education while girls would have to stay home to learn culinary skills.

As a teacher and coach, this project was an amazing opportunity, to give back to others what we here take for granted. Even now, in Pakistan and all around third-world countries, there are still so many children unable to be educated and projects like this only take one person to come up with an idea and get in touch with the right people, to make it happen.

By the end of 2021, we had a refurbished college and a technology lab for the students. This is how things are done. Ideas are created in the mind, circulated within our world/universe and brought back to us at the correct time. Hope and faith prevail knowing that all dreams can come true. We just need to become the right person when the opportunity arises.

It wasn't all easy. I was known for being outspoken at times but when the microphone was presented to me, I froze. This shocked me more than a few other people that thought they knew me. I would and could easily stand in class and give a speech on life lessons and sometimes, world politics, but when I was asked to go on stage to do something similar, I would step back. I am sometimes reminded of these times by my colleagues, friends and family, which always motivates me in my current journey of the self. The journey of my dreams and goals, which have grown over time, are now clearer to me.

I got rid of these fears - What will people say? What will they think? What if they don't like me? All of these had to go if I was to achieve my best.

My intentions and goals are connected to a higher purpose and I remind myself all the time, the *outcome doesn't matter, what matters is the person you become in the process.* The harsh reality is, we may or may not be around to see the results, so why ponder over what is uncertain? Be who you are, and who you want to be, and take the opportunities that come your way to make you a better version of yourself.

Throughout lockdown, I decided I had to achieve my higher level in coaching and therapy, so worked towards and achieved a master's practitioner by 2021. By then, I was already planning my future profession as a community events organiser, radio presenter/host and even one day standing on stage to deliver my Personal Development Program, in a centre where I will have some say in, what goes on and what types of sessions we would carry out.

I made nearly every day productive, knowing that whatever happened, I wanted to be ready for the opportunities when they came to me. As I joined group sessions for my growth, I realised I was not alone in my journey and all I needed was an opportunity to prove my abilities. The group sessions were amazing and as a client, we were always given lots of tools to work on ourselves, to be the better edition of ourselves.

We all used this space to share worries and concerns. We took our learnings, implemented them and shared them. I am working on my group coaching clients in this way and know that this kind of support is not always available. These openings, when taken, can change and transform you so you love yourself enough to withstand what others think. You love that you are an individual and this makes you whole. No amount of praise, loving affirmations and gifts make up for this and only you can achieve what is best for you. Only you have envisioned your goals and have knowledge that you will achieve them.

I took no chances, I enrolled in short courses to teach me what I needed to become a leader in the education sector.

The level 5 certificate in leadership, has played a big part in my confidence, as I know now that I see myself as a leader.

As we came out of lockdown, everything fell into place. I was assured as a single mum, I was secure in my house. I thank the Almighty every day for this and know that we should take nothing for granted. The marriage breakdown led to legal issues and meetings that I had made sure I was prepared for. This helped me immensely to achieve my status as a mum and the lead role in my small family.

I had to stay focused on my children and home now, to make it as comfortable as I could, even though the home had been torn and mended, leaving visible cracks. My three beautiful children are my world. Loving, caring and nurturing them feels unreal, they always remind me that I am their best friend... until they get told off. Sometimes, they'll reassure me that I am whatever they want me to be, and other times we have a disagreement that turns into a tantrum on both sides. I know that we are not all perfect and we will all sometimes make mistakes. Knowing this and accepting that even we adults can make mistakes keeps you humble and strongly connected as a family.

Some Tips I learnt along the way, and I am still learning, are:

Don't take anything personally.

End an argument with an apology and move on quickly, because indeed life is too short and the seconds tick faster every day.

Cherish every moment with your parents and family, as you never know when it can be taken from you.

I know I appreciate my parents and siblings more now than ever - the kind words, the endless, emotional and physical support and the constant reminders that they are always there for me no matter what. This was always there, but there were times when judgements were clouded by negative emotions and this would come in the way of my appreciation for their love.

Know that you'll face ups and downs, and the emotions will come and go. You will not escape from these, as we are human. We are facing issues all the time and the learning comes when we accept that the emotions have taken over our clarity and our focus and we lose the ability to even prepare dinner. This will lead to overthinking and even going on autopilot, where we are not able to drive consciously because our minds will drift to the negative.

You will become empowered, resilient and able to help others, once you can identify yourself as in need of help.

I went to my therapist, at the last hurdle, when I felt I could take no more of the naysayers. Comments directed at me may have been made with positive intentions but felt like an attack every time. I was taking things personally. I was feeling vulnerable. When my marriage broke up, the realisation of being left alone to look after three kids was overpowering - knowing that the future path needed me to be strong and motivated so I could be a positive role model for my children was overwhelming.

When I found myself on the sacred prayer mat, asking to be taken from the cruel world, I knew then that I was becoming spiritually, mentally and physically weak. This was all down to my emotions taking over my heart and mind. There were times when I was able to complete tasks because I had to and there were times I was frozen to the spot. I knew what I needed and felt for the first time a fear of coming out of my mind's closet.

I was already in contact with my guru, coach and therapist and we both knew it was time. My mind was a rollercoaster, of wins and losses, looking for ways to find closed boxes in the mind, that I never knew were there.

We explored the level that is not attainable on a conscious level. The knowledge that I was holding of very old emotions was causing pain in my body, as there was no way of releasing them. There was no action from me before the sessions to express, release and share deep emotions, so this prospect was remarkable. After what felt like a gazillion sessions, I felt able to shift them. I was not left alone. A good rapport with your therapist and a relationship of trust, love and respect holds a huge advantage, as you're able to call them as and when, or leave them a message, knowing that they will treat you with respect by keeping it all confidential. This level of trust was not possible for me before as, apart from my parents and siblings, I couldn't trust anyone. I knew at that point, sometimes to release negativity, you had to trust, become vulnerable and open up to them. This is the only way to get the help that you need.

I have taken up several opportunities since the lockdown as I had used the lockdown period to upskill my learning, even joining an international platform that was made available virtually. This shows that you can invest your time productively. Sometimes you will feel fear and the nerves will create a block. Know that it's natural to feel like this when you are leaving your comfort zone to join one that requires responsibility, control of emotions and even practical thinking. You can use the online platform as a safe space to gain knowledge as well as share content. Know that there are precautions to take and you should take time out to go over the content because you are opening yourself to a world of opportunities, as well as those that may look for anything to negatively point at.

I took up opportunities that I used to say no to and even offered my services to organisations where I spoke to women and young people about self-development. Recently, I have written a message to the local university to offer a group coaching session. As a client, I am always told, believe in what you have and what you can achieve and you will be the best.

When I first arrived in the new city, I felt nervous. I knew that it would be a tough feat, but it would be an adventure just the same and I would get to know more people. I was blessed to be surrounded by people that could understand my perspective and would be able to work alongside me to help create a thriving community.

I got in touch with local community organisations and we built rapport quite quickly -and after nine years we are still working together to help in whichever way we can support our people - they need more than just benefits and welfare, they needed activities and socialising. More recently, we have managed to create an open space for women to come and share their concerns, knowing that they're in a safe environment.

I play many roles in the community now and although they are not all full-time roles, I hold a title for each one. This would not have been possible had I not been able to reach out and ask for the much-needed support. I was at my lowest and have now reached a level where I still feel I can grow. The fear does come and sometimes it leads me to be distracted and overthink, however, powerful tools as a coach and a teacher, self-talk and a regular check-in with myself work wonders. If you need help, always reach out, and know that someone, somewhere is there just for you, waiting for you to take the first step and say yes to inner change.

Know that Pain and Suffering are not forever. You may, one day, be tested in ways that you never thought possible but believe that you have a whole universe inside as do the people around us. Everyone has their model of the world and will treat you differently. Stay around for the good times and get support at your less easy times. Be there for others when you can and hold healthy boundaries where you feel content and are willing to be a listener, consoler and reassurer when needed.

About the Author
SALMA ZHAID

Salma Zhaid is a Community Events Organiser and Part-time teacher in Derby, UK.

She holds coffee mornings, to provide a safe space for the local women, they can go and share concerns or just enjoy each other's company. This space also offers her coaching services in person or online.

She wants to make a bigger difference by creating more skills workshops and offer help where the women need, regarding home life, including; parenting, relationships and even Career Coaching, to anyone over 14 years.

Salma Zhaid is also running a Coaching business online and

offers women programs that help to break barriers within to achieve the best of themselves. She qualified in 2021 as Master NLP, Timeline and Hypnotherapy Practitioner. So, subscribe online for her latest courses to improve self-development. These are all offered online and in person, so get in touch to gain more information.

She loves to Socialise at Community Events and Read Books.

You Can Reach Salma Zhaid at:

Email: annisacoaching@yahoo.com

Website: www.annisacoaching.com

facebook.com/salma.zhaid
instagram.com/an.nisa.coaching

CHAPTER 7
NO RISK, NO MAGIC!
SANAM HUSSAIN

"Did we not expand for you, [O Muhammad] your chest?
And we removed from you your burden
Which had weighed upon your back
And raised high for you your reputation.
For indeed with hardship [will be] ease
Certainly, with difficulty [will be] ease...
So when you have finished, devote yourself to Allah's worship.
And to your Lord turn intentions and hopes."

— QURAN; 94 1-8

NO RISK, NO MAGIC!

We all go through various life experiences and wonder why this is happening to us, *"Why me?"* or, *"Can I get a break?"*, but this thinking puts you on the effect side of the equation, which means you've energetically given up all accountability and personal power.

Have you ever felt that deep-sinking feeling in your heart? You ask yourself: Who are you? Why are you here? How do you fit into the world? What is the reason behind spending so many years of your life serving everyone else's needs but YOUR OWN? You feel deep regret and lack confidence about what you want. You feel stuck in a dark sinking hole - does no one hear your voice? That silent sense of crying in your heart?

That was me, the sixteen-year-old who went through an identical crisis and challenging time. But through it all, one thing remained - TAWAKUL on ALLAH [the reliance on GOD] was still alive, and that is what motivated me to keep going to reach the light at the end of a dark tunnel. I've learned to listen to my instincts - the gut feelings that keep telling me there's more to come.

I was a British Pakistani Muslim little girl who was born and raised in Pakistan, despite my mother being a British citizen.

My mother, who built her whole life in Pakistan with my father, knew she had all the right to live the way she wanted. My mom always taught me that every believer should believe in Allah and know Allah is the best planner. And whenever you question your fate and ask "Why me?", the answer is straightforward; it is never luck or fortune. It's Allah's perfect plan!

> "They plan, and Allah plans. Surely, Allah is the best of planners."
>
> — QURAN, 8:30

Have you ever doubted your own abilities? How did it affect you?

I felt lost, confused, broken, betrayed, bullied, exhausted, and emotionally blackmailed.

You get broken down to rock bottom at some point in your Life. This is because Allah, The Most High, is experimenting with your life. It's not that he hates you; God often puts to trial those whom he loves. The King of the kings is trying to see your sincerity, patience, reliance, and steadfastness. He puts you through those difficulties because He knows something better is in store for you. So, when your trial comes, remember that no one will be able to bail you out except Him - The One Who put you in that situation.

When I was younger, I was good at leading people and loved helping others. I especially liked helping girls who were being bullied and making them feel strong in the areas where they felt weak. Many of the girls I helped had a hard time because of how things were in their culture and society. Some didn't get much help from their parents or teachers, who thought it was okay to use physical punishment to make them behave. I worked hard to help the girls feel strong and do well in their studies. I allowed them to practice for tests and exams to get good grades like me. It makes me feel thrilled to see them succeed!

I had a great childhood, along with my brother and sisters. I was the eldest of the siblings and my parents were thrilled that I always achieved high marks at school, setting a good example for the others - what more could a middle-class parent ask for?

I had so many dreams for the future and saw myself being well educated, having a great job earning loads of money, getting married and living the best, happiest life ever after. Still, there was part of me that felt uneasy and insecure about things - as if something terrible was about to happen that was beyond my control. I was confused.

Then, one day, it happened. My feelings of anxiety were realised. My mother shouted my name when I was ready to make my first prayer of the day at fajr time [dawn prayer] in the early morning, after performing my ablutions. She needed to talk about something important. I was just a normal person, sitting at the breakfast table when she broke the news that I was getting married. I thought she was joking, trying to teach me to be well responsible towards my duties because my life would soon change, and I should be more focused on house chores than studying, but she wasn't joking. After hearing all of this, something instantly earth-shattering happened to me.

My entire world had turned into resentment at that point. I was in year eleven, only two months away from my exams. My inner child was confused, surrounded by laughter and love from my family and yet having to deal with evolving into a naive young lady, passionate about having grand ambitions, well-educated, and whose aspirations now seemed to be crumbling into bits.

I was a young British Pakistani Muslim who married early, and I was becoming a young woman of Pakistani descent. I moved to the UK from another nation to start a new life full of obstacles and challenging experiences. Because I did not speak the language fluently, I experienced a loss of self-confidence. That young girl inside me was now screaming for a door to open and a way to succeed.

Have you ever lost confidence in yourself? And how did it make you feel?

You shouldn't only rely on life to turn out the way YOU want it to. You assume it will go smoothly, slipping right from under your feet. You start to uncover that you can succeed by trusting Allah.

In the first year of my marriage, I was blessed with my first-born daughter and soon, I was pregnant again with my son. My future path to success came to a halt and I embraced the role of a sister-in-law, a daughter-in-law, a wife and a mother of two.

While my husband was supportive, my lack of confidence, the upheaval from my home and all the changes I'd seen led me to postnatal depression. I became a mother of two in my teens while striving for independence to be able to devote time to my own success. Through the years, I have been deprived of power over my life due to circumstances and had no power to change things. I have felt like I have had fingers pointed at me and doubts raised about my ability to be a good mother, wife and daughter-in-law because I wanted more for myself and I felt that any time I tried to cross the line from housewife to businesswoman, I was put down. I never lost faith though. I believed there was something more, even if I couldn't figure it out.

Let me ask you a question: do you ever feel that you don't fit in and go out of your way to pretend to be like people around you, even though you're terrified deep down?

At the age of 23, after seven years on the rollercoaster, the race was about to end and I went home to visit my family. I was thrilled to finally see my parents, siblings, and especially my dearest friend, my mum. I was such a mama's baby girl. I still remember when my mother was waiting impatiently at the door to welcome my three beautiful kids, two daughters and a son, and everything seemed like a dream to me. I went for two months and spent a lot of time with my family. Suddenly, my health began to deteriorate; I was having difficulty walking and moving around due to a back condition, and I was expecting my fourth baby boy. Praise be to God.

> "Sufficient for us is Allah, and [He is] the best Wakeel [disposer of affairs]."
>
> — QURAN 3:173

Thankfully, I was in good hands. My mother decided to look after my third child, who was only nine months of age. It was the best decision I ever made.

Leaving my child in Pakistan with my mum and returning to the UK was difficult for me. Coming back was like leaving my soul hundreds of miles behind. On the other side, there was a storm brewing that I couldn't bear. I was labelled as selfish, a bad mother, and reckless. I was unable to walk due to a herniated disc in my lower back, so I was already in a poor physical state, but deep down, emotionally I began to feel guilty and embarrassed. I hated myself for abandoning my kid.

I was now at the age of 24, a mother of four children and experiencing a lack of energy. I felt tired all the time, had trouble sleeping at night, had difficulty bonding with my babies, and had problems concentrating and making decisions. I had frightening thoughts because I allowed my emotions to take over and my thoughts began to explode out of control.

After giving birth to four amazing children and putting up with a tremendous lot of unsettling behaviour over several years, I found myself in dark days of sorrow and anxiety. I started believing I was not good enough, which made me feel bad about myself.

There was no way in my life to say no. I was constantly exhausting myself and had no boundaries in trying to please everyone. Because of my low self-esteem, I put up with others taking advantage of me.

That's what Allah had planned for me. One day, when I was tired of feeling the emptiness and deep sadness, fear, and heartbreak, I remembered what Allah says in Quran!

"INDEED, ALLAH WILL NOT CHANGE THE CONDITION OF A PEOPLE UNTIL THEY CHANGE WHAT IS IN THEMSELVES."

— QURAN [13:11]

I remember scrolling through Instagram, looking for positive wisdom quotes that could support me so I could restart my normal, peaceful lifestyle. I had a light-bulb moment when I realised I could no longer go without help and then found this:

> "The first step towards getting somewhere is to decide that you are not going to stay where you are."
>
> — J.P. MORGAN

I know you have been through a lot in your life, sis. Most of us have gone through times like this. Instead of behaving genuinely, we tell people what we think they want to hear and act in ways that go against our true nature. In short, we're living inauthentically.

Fall in love with the process of becoming the best version of yourself.

If you are reading this chapter, understand - IT'S GOING TO BE OKAY!

Trust the plan of Allah. He is the best planner. Praise be to God. Keep on going. It all works out IN SHA ALLAH.

After the birth of my son and my health recovery, my husband's fantastic support enabled me to begin my own personal journey of healing. Excellent professionals guided me through therapy and healing breakthroughs. It was time to go deep and let go of all the memories and feelings holding me back from becoming who I truly was. Like an onion, I removed the layers of myself until I found the real me.

The Tao the Chin says!

> "Knowing others is intelligence; knowing yourself is true wisdom. Mastering others is strength; mastering yourself is true power. If you realise that you have enough, you are truly rich."

Knowing SELF Needs a Knife to Cut Through the Tough initial Layer.

So why do we require self-awareness?

Let's start with some challenging questions.

- How much do you know about your daily work?
- How well do you understand your parents?
- How well do you know your partner?
- Now, please tell me how well you know yourself.
- You could feel more anxious about the last question than the others.

We are often so concerned with the lives of others that we forget to look in the mirror and talk to ourselves. Unfortunately, we have lost the value of solitude and self-talk in connecting with ourselves.

A QUICK TEST!

Close your eyes for a moment and try to visualise your face.

It will not be a simple task.

Why?

Because we rarely see ourselves in that way.

Mirrors have become a tool for looking gorgeous while not feeling fabulous.

Knowing yourself is challenging, however, it's also not difficult.

Knowing yourself is the first step towards a beautiful and happy life because you realise you are beyond what you believe when you understand SELF.

In this chapter, I will provide life-changing knowledge to help you transform your viewpoint and truly understand yourself.

Human brains are incredibly strong. We may educate our thoughts to work either for us or against us. Most people go through life without realizing how powerful the brain is and how it can shape your Life to be as perfect as you want it to be, by the will of Allah.

There's a unique world living inside you and, like all beautiful adventures, diving into yourself can be scary. It needs you to confront your fears, habits and other's beliefs that have been holding you back from childhood.

I started working on myself through ongoing study and unlocking new doors towards self-discovery that brought my continuous effort to fruition. I can now show the world how easy it is to Empower yourself by working on the Mindset.

As a Certified, Trauma Informed Master practitioner of NLP Master Practitioner of Time Line Therapy and Hypnotherapy, I have mastered and used the most effective principles and techniques to help me transform my life. Through the same procedures I'm sharing with you, I've also been able to help my family and clients change their lives.

Before I go any further, I'd like to share some insights from my Time Line Therapy session with one of my fantastic clients.

> "Working with Sanam has been amazing. She's such a kind soul and has a very caring and gentle approach.
>
> My sessions with Sanam have been brilliant. I was able to release negative emotions and limiting beliefs that I had since childhood. She was able to help me release anxiety, too, which has helped me with so many positive changes in my life.
>
> Thank you Sanam xx"

I'll share some principles that helped me change my Life.

The following are **the Presuppositions of NLP**. NLP is so powerful. I've studied it myself, I'm using it at home for my children, and I'm using it for my clients. It's unique, and there are so many techniques that are going to help so many women.

THE PRESUPPOSITIONS OF NLP

1. **People** have all the resources they need to succeed and achieve their desired outcomes (There are no unresourceful people, only unresourceful states).
2. **Respect** for the other person's model of the world.
3. **Everyone** is doing their best with the resources available at that time (Behaviour is geared for adaptation, and the present behaviour is the best choice available Every behaviour is motivated by a positive intent).
4. **Signs** of resistance in a client is a sign of a lack of rapport (There are no resistant clients, only inflexible communicators. Effective communicators accept and utilise all communication presented to them).
5. **U** are in charge of your mind and, therefore, your results (I am also in charge of my mind and, therefore, my results).
6. **Procedures** should always be designed to increase wholeness.
7. **Procedures** should always be designed to increase choice.
8. **Observe** and calibrate [notice and adjust] behaviour: The most important information about a person is their behaviour.

9. <u>S</u>ystem - The person with the most flexibility of behaviour will control the system - The Law of Requisite Variety.
10. <u>I</u>nterpret and evaluate all behaviour and change in terms of context and ecology.
11. <u>T</u>he Map is not the Territory (The words that we use are NOT the event or the item they represent).
12. <u>I</u>n Communication - Your communication's meaning is the response you get.
13. <u>O</u>nly Feedback! - There is no failure, only feedback.
14. <u>N</u>ot their Behaviour - People are not their behaviours (Accept the person; change the Behaviour).

HOW TO BUILD A HEALTHY SELF-RELATIONSHIP DAILY BASIS

One of the most critical relationships you'll ever have is with yourself. Here is how to nurture it.

When you hear "relationship," you probably think of your relationships and behaviour with others, such as a family member, parents, partner, or friend.

Let's be honest, we also have a significant connection with ourselves. One of the most important relationships we'll ever have is with ourselves and how we think about and treat ourselves is important.

WHAT REALLY IS A SELF-RELATIONSHIP?

In the simplest form imaginable, a self-relationship is what it looks like and feels like to have a relationship you have with yourself. It includes how you treat yourself, the choices you make about yourself, and how you think about yourself. Or, to put it another way, it's how we perceive, understand, engage with, and pay attention to our needs. It's how we feel about every aspect of who we are, including our bodies, feelings, thoughts, and behaviour. And it's how we treat those elements of ourselves, whether with love, encouragement and compassion or with judgement and hatred.

WHY IS IT VITAL TO HAVE A SELF-RELATIONSHIP?

It may seem strange to have one because, as a south Asian culture, we are not mentally built in a way to know the importance of **"self-love and care"**. Being judgmental of yourself, for example, can hurt your self-esteem, causing you to feel horrible about yourself regularly. Low self-esteem may cause you to isolate or avoid family and friends. It may cause you to lose your boundaries with others, allowing destructive situations into your life.

Over time, this can affect your relationships with people, your confidence at work, and your desire to achieve your own goals.

Wouldn't it be amazing to understand and take care of yourself by letting go of limiting beliefs and placing your worth with love?

Here are some tips to enhance the bond with yourself!

1. Check in with yourself!

2. Validate all your feelings!

3. Remember that it is perfectly okay to say "**NO!**"

4. Find time for yourself and the things you love to do at your favourite time!

5. Set boundaries!

6. Remind yourself that caring for yourself is not "**selfish!**"

7. Think about writing in a journal!

8. Every day, try to think of positive affirmations about yourself, such as:

I am enough because I know my self-worth!

I Love Myself unconditionally before anyone else loves me!

9. Have gratitude for being alive, for **You Are a gift** in this world. Remember Allah in all conditions!

HERE IS ANOTHER DOSE OF REALITY!

When you focus your decisions on what other people think, you are looking for approval, praise and acceptance. Please take a moment to focus on your emotions when you find yourself in this situation. Observe the feeling and ask yourself what is coming up for me. Repeat your techniques each time it happens. If a particular emotion keeps coming up, it must be acknowledged. You won't need the approval of others once you get the root cause of the emotion recognised and resolved. You might not have received it as a kid and are now seeking it in adulthood.

When I used to rely on other people's thoughts and decisions, I was constantly used to seeking validation. I used to come up with undesirable emotions like anger, sadness, fear, and guilt. I used to cause more conflict and emotional hurt by not getting enough **love and respect** from another person. I believed the actual meaning of life was to receive love from others. Accepting my feelings and judgements about myself led me to learn to validate myself in my world.

Allah uses broken things beautifully, Be kind to your heart and stop worrying about something you can't control. Let Allah handle it because Allah knows you are tired and you are still trying, and He knows it's difficult for you. Remember that Allah will never give you a burden that you can't handle.

" الحياة **Remind yourself, Life is a Test.**"

When I look back and see how I was versus the empowered woman I am now, I have come so far that I should pat myself on the back. Life now is much more beautiful than I could ever have imagined. I wish I had known this before. However, after becoming the cycle breaker, I can create a safe space for my children as a calm parent. This gives me the reason to live to the best of each moment, by the will of Allah. It is so amazing when you start deeply loving yourself more. You are in a win-win situation

Do you want to know more about HOW you can change your life?

CONNECTING WITH YOUR INNER POWER!

Would you agree if I said that 90% of the mind is unconscious and 10% is conscious? Would you believe that the conscious mind is the GOAL SETTER and the unconscious mind is the GOAL GETTER?

COMMUNICATION WITHOUT BEING AWARE UNCONSCIOUSLY.

To show the importance of unconscious cognition, imagine I asked you, "Would you kindly tell me where you were born?" How would you respond? Perhaps the location's name? How would you react to the same question if you were in a deeper level of trance and I was speaking to your Unconscious Mind? The answer is "Yes," or nod. That is the correct answer. It's a fantastic example of the unconscious mind taking things seriously.

WHY IS UNCONSCIOUS INTELLIGENCE ESSENTIAL?

How we think, behave and speak can help us specify what will happen in our external world. Ask yourself, are the results you have achieved in life, relationships, family, health, business/career and money consistent with the goals you've established so far? If you said NO, then your conscious efforts conflict with your unconscious self. It is about internal self-awareness of the current moment, disconnecting from negative emotions, and making decisions based on past events.

I use Time Line Therapy® to detach your unconscious mind from negative emotions of self-limiting beliefs that could prevent you from achieving a life of great wholeness and success. There will be less conflict and more options available to you now to learn from your past experiences that were once not there.

CONNECTING WITH YOUR INNER SELF!

Once negative emotions and limiting decisions have been removed using Time Line Therapy®, You can see, hear, and feel your surroundings with clarity and peace. Looking at the past from a different perspective connects you with your inner self much more freely.

CHILDHOOD TRAUMAS!

I know you've been through a lot in your life, but most problems go back to childhood experiences because up to the age of seven, we absorb our parents' and families' emotions, thoughts and feelings. At that age, we unconsciously decide how we will now interact with older people.

Do you ever feel rushed to become an adult and bombarded by life's pressures so you've disconnected from your childhood?

DID YOU KNOW YOU HAVE AN INNER CHILD?

Every person has an inner child who has been with them since conception. Your inner child has carried you through all phases of life and continues to exist within you.

Early childhood trauma can be especially harmful. Early childhood trauma is experienced as trauma occurring between birth and seven. A child's brain grows and develops rapidly, especially during the first three years. Young children also rely on carers for care, nurturing, and protection. Early childhood trauma can have an impact on a child's development.

Trauma can make young children especially vulnerable. When trauma occurs early, it can affect a child's development. It can also affect their ability to attach securely, mainly when trauma occurs with a caregiver.

HOW DO YOU KNOW IF YOU HAD CHILDHOOD TRAUMA?

You may struggle with trust, have low self-esteem, judge fear, constantly try to please others, have outbursts of frustration, or suffer from constant social anxiety.

WHAT ARE THE SIGNS OF ADULT CHILDHOOD TRAUMA?

Adult symptoms of childhood trauma

- Anger.
- Unresponsiveness.
- Anxiety.
- Excessive emotion.
- Depression.
- Panic attacks.

I have mentioned NLP in the section above about **The Presuppositions of NeuroLinguistic programming**. NLP is a method for modelling excellence. These presuppositions are not beliefs or laws and are not regulating rules or regulations. They are the mindsets that lead to achievement.

It clarifies how you may quickly change your perspective to see the best in yourself and others.

HERE ARE SOME PRACTICAL WAYS OF RECONNECTING WITH YOUR INNER CHILD!

- Reassure yourself and your inner child by telling yourself that you are secure and loved.
- Accept the emotions you are encountering and let them go.
- Practise setting healthy boundaries.
- Practice self-care and treat yourself like you would treat your child.
- Start gratitude journaling.
- Listen to your body.
- Keep your promises to yourself.
- Write a letter to yourself - your younger self.

It's incredibly beneficial to write a letter to your inner child.

Write your name at the top and start with Dear_____ (your name).

Focus on what your inner child wants to hear and the comfort needed from you. **Reparent your inner child** by using the letter-writing technique. Make sure you are writing with an accurate hand.

Are you a right- or left-handed person?

Do you want to know your younger self? If you are a right-handed person, your left hand represents you, and if you are a left-handed person, your right hand represents you.

As a framework, ask yourself the following questions.

How do you feel?

How can I help you?

What do you require right now?

Forgive yourself, love yourself, and be kind to yourself. You can repeat this practice each time to coach yourself whenever any emotion comes up for you, then do this exercise.

REMEMBER, YOU ARE UNIQUE; YOU OWN YOUR POWER!

I can not imagine closing off my chapter like this.

I'm on top of the world for all of you reading my story right now; it is honestly unbelievable.

I am dedicating this chapter to my beautiful kids, Safa, Adam, Marwa, and Yousaf, who have been patient in the whole process of writing, especially Safa, my eldest [15], who has been there for me as an immense support throughout my most challenging times, looking after her younger siblings. I am sending her loads of love.

Big thanks to my mom and sister Swaira, They have always been emotionally available to encourage me to move forward. My Love for Umrah [my niece] is above and beyond for her patience in eagerly waiting for me to receive kisses and cuddles.

She successfully discovered her road, silently dropped out of the competition she never wanted to enter, and then continued to victory, empowering many others on her journey. She is enthusiastic about sharing her experience and how her path led her to where she is able to train women to shift their mindset and master their emotions.

Dear readers,

As you come to the end of this chapter, I want to leave you with a powerful message that I hope will stick with you: "**No Risk, No Magic.**" This phrase is more than just a catchy title for the chapter—it's A chant for living a fulfilling and meaningful life.

We are often held back by fear of failing or hesitation to try anything new. But we can only find our potential and experience life's mystery by taking chances. Taking chances is crucial to development and success, whether pursuing a new job, establishing a business, or embarking on a new journey.

Of course, taking risks doesn't mean being reckless or irresponsible. It means stepping outside your comfort zone and facing the unknown, even when it's scary or unclear. It means embracing the possibility of failure and using it as a learning opportunity.

So as you go forward from this chapter, I encourage you to keep this phrase in your mind "No Risk, No Magic" Take chances, be bold, and see where it takes you. Who knows what magic awaits?

Good luck, Sanam.

About the Author
SANAM HUSSAIN

Sanam is a mindset coach. She has completed extensive training in Neuro-Linguistic Programming (NLP), Time Line Therapy, and Hypnotherapy. And a certified Trauma

Informed Master practitioner of NLP, Master Practitioner of Time Line Therapy and Hypnotherapy with experience helping women overcome emotional challenges.

She has also received specific training in trauma-informed care, which allows her to approach her work with empathy and a deep understanding of how trauma affects the brain and body.

She specializes in working with clients who have experienced trauma and uses Time Line Therapy techniques to support healing and personal growth.

She is passionate about helping women lead more satisfying and meaningful lives.

Here you can approach her:

Contact: 07534420772

Email: sanamsymir12@yahoo.com

facebook.com/Sanam%20Hussain

CHAPTER 8
THE PILGRIMAGE WITHIN
UMM SADIQ

October has always been my favourite month because of the colours, the leaves falling, and a real sense of healing, letting go and regrowth. It was a Wednesday morning in October when I realised, I wanted to be a coach.

It feels like I was in a personal development program yesterday when I had to visualise my ideal day. For me, this was a moment of epiphany. Fast forward to now, and I'm living that moment. I hold this memory in gratitude whilst looking at the sheep from the window in the cottage I'm staying in. My soul knows that the aim was - and still is - to know myself. Knowing myself was the only way to know my Lord intimately. I want to be with my Lord. I now see that I am on a mission to help myself and others to stay connected with their fitra (natural disposition) and Allah by letting go of the blocks and obstacles in the way.

Every day, I ask myself, "are you dying or growing?" And the answer is always, resoundingly, growing. I know now that the more I learn, the more there is to learn. Growth surrounds me, and mental comfort for me is the death of growing. Staying put is no longer an option. No matter how much I grow, my desire to keep growing grows along with it. The aim is to keep expanding my level of consciousness. There is no limit, for Allah is endless.

Allah has placed in each one of us a 'sir' (personal secret), something much more potent than potential. Most go through life without being aware of this and lose out on the abundance that awaits them. In essence, accessing this 'sir' requires growth, a level of consciousness that allows for the purification of your soul. Intention alone is not enough; it must be supported by action and faith. Growth is only possible with conscious healing work.

Being the eldest child, there were many expectations exclusively for me. I effectively ended up parenting my parents and siblings despite not having the skills to parent anyone. Culturally, not being a firstborn boy also brought its own challenges. I had to prove to the world that I was as good as any boy. I was a cheeky tomboy, and most found me to be very determined. Did I feel determined? Yes, but it wasn't fuelled by positivity. I was trying to prove to society and those around me that I was invincible.

Having worked on myself and learning how positive and negative drivers propel us, I now ensure that I work from a place of positive motivation, but I didn't know this back then. I was a girl living with the expectations that came from a boy. I had to prove I was looking after myself, my siblings, and my parents.

Like most brown children, I was expected to become a lawyer, but I wanted something else. Internally, I felt a sense of injustice. I had been planning my choice of career since I was thirteen, but I knew I had to do what my parents wanted. I had to make them proud. I remember my Grandad saying to me before he passed away how proud of me, he was. He valued education as he never had one, and I had fulfilled his dream. I now realise I had much generational trauma to release to attain my desired life. Someone had to be the changemaker; I am grateful that someone was me.

I have always had a strong intuition about things and people, but when it came to me, I ignored it. Not a wise move. Law was one of those situations. After the initial glitz and glamour, I knew it wasn't for me. Though successful at work, weekends were waves of sadness, and the pressure crumbled me internally. I tried to reassure myself that helping people and doing lots of pro bono work was compensating for my career, but this was not satisfying me. Still, while I was outwardly successful, I was internally deeply unfulfilled.

A few years later, I lost my Grandad. He was my go-to person, best friend, guide, and rock. The ache and loneliness were deep. I was so emotional yet closed off. I remember sitting with my family and thinking, either I will die on you, or you will die on me. I wanted to protect myself from that pain and others too. I was unaware at that time that death is a beautiful gift, a reunion of souls departed, and something to celebrate whilst grieving. I decided loving someone was too painful and would no longer love a new person again. There was no space for new love.

Initially, to deal with this loss, I turned to my faith. This was the legacy my Grandad had left for his family. I loved learning what I was learning and enjoyed this transformation, but, like all transformations, the deeper level comes after the surface layer has been peeled back. This required much more conscious inner healing. Spirituality does not only happen on a prayer mat. I was trying to align my life without knowing who I was or what I valued. The following years saw moments of anxiety and deep depression. I often felt like a failure and did not know what I wanted to do with my life. Anxiety had become my best friend and my new comfort zone. Being an empath, I felt things before processing them, and anxiety often appeared in the in-between stage. Now I welcome it. It's a messenger telling me that either I or circumstances are out of alignment with my core self.

Losing my Grandad did spur me to leave law, but I felt like a massive failure once I was out of it. When you want to change, somebody or something will test your sincerity. I was being offered lucrative opportunities in law, including partnerships.

Everyone around me thought I was mad. Who leaves a career with status and money that they have worked so hard to attain? But I had such deep sadness and knew I had to change. I was gifted naturally by God's grace, but gifts also require action to materialise.

Throughout university, I had a full-time job. I was a high performer and left university practically debt free, but here I was now, with no job. Those six months of my life were the hardest. Whenever I had to go to 'sign on', I felt like a failure. I remember sitting there in tears. On one occasion, the officer responsible for me was affected by my state and decided to quote verses from the Quran. He told me to read the pre-dawn prayer. What he did not know was that I was already doing all that. It wasn't that I was distanced from my faith – I was very connected, but I had deep-rooted trauma presenting itself and it was now ready to be released. If I spoke to my younger self now, I would say, "hang in there, lovely; things do get better. Once I took the path to heal, I never looked back."

I was told I was adorable and cheeky from a very young age. This became my mask. Behind the cover was a very insecure woman. I recognised my strength was dealing with other people's crises, but my cup was empty in the process. I was seen as a confident, determined individual. My CV began with this. I faked it well professionally. The truth was I had imposter syndrome. I did not feel good enough.

From the age of fifteen, I suffered panic attacks, and on one family trip, due to all the emotions around me, my limbs gave way, and I ended up in a wheelchair. My body was unable to hold itself together. I realised that the type of empath I was, I needed to make sure I took time out for my self-care. I loved writing, but journaling and brain-dumping had never crossed my mind back then. Now I can ask deep, powerful questions of myself to regulate my emotions.

Before healing, I was on a journey of self-sabotage. As I mentioned before, my life consisted of working Monday to Friday and then crumbling at the weekend. I had the fear that I would be exposed. I needed to take time out to recalibrate, but instead, I burnt out. Irrational thoughts consumed me. I feared success. I thought failure was my destiny, and that everyone around me was looking down on me. I feared I would be ridiculed. This fear stopped me from taking opportunities to grow. I believed life was hard, and I had worked hard to get where I was, and this was enough. I didn't need to go any further. I was safer here, so why would I risk stepping out? Every time something went wrong, I blamed myself. It was a punishment for x, y or z. I forgot significant achievements, like kissing the black stone because I felt unworthy. Back then, I was not enough.

I was very lonely. Nobody understood me. The more I tried explaining what was happening, the more they didn't understand me. This made me feel even more unworthy. Their model of the world was different to mine. We didn't speak about mental health and would pretend everything was ok. I believed every negative comment that was sent my way. I internalised everything that everyone said to me. Half-truths started to become my reality. I started shying away from social gatherings and friends. I felt I had nothing to offer. They all had perfect lives in my eyes, and I felt out of place. Slowly, I started losing friends. I was very prickly, yet I longed to be loved. I was trying to get them to see my model of the world, but instead, I was becoming more and more misunderstood. I now know you must respect everyone's model of the world without imposing your own on them. You cannot make others see what they are unaware of or unwilling to see. The unconscious mind suppresses what it is not ready to deal with. Mine was prepared, which is why things presented themselves to heal, allowing me to move on and live the life I desire. I am so grateful for this now.

I also had severe body dysmorphia. I worked out twice a day and felt like I was obese. Even today, I talked about this to a loved one, and she did not understand. In her eyes, I was slim, but in my world, I looked awful. I hated how I looked. I remember going for meals and excusing myself in between courses to exercise in the restroom. When I look at pictures of myself from back then, I see a beautiful but sad woman, and I often tell her that she is simply perfect. This was her journey, and I am thankful to her for taking the steps she did so I become the woman I am now.

Life has been a journey with many moments of change. I often reached these moments but then continued with old unresourceful patterns. I reached out to coaches, psychotherapists, scholars and the like, but I still needed to commit to real change. It made me feel better in the short term, but I did not take the opportunity to have profound transformational changes. The chaos built up again but quicker this time, as there was already a route in my mind to build upon.

I had a history of burning out, like most high performers. I was the queen of masking, and my family honestly did not know the extent of my anxiety and depression. My thoughts were so intrusive that they affected every area of my life. I found some relief in studying my faith, but my intrusive thoughts even took over there. I was consumed with fear, yet to the world, I was successful. I had a career that most only dreamed of, but I wasn't happy. Where once I craved status, money, fast cars and houses, none of this mattered anymore. I sought healing from all over the place. It was a journey that took me to Jordan, Al Aqsa, Makkah and Madinah, yet, after the short-lived relief, I ended up again, full of anxiety and depression.

One day, over lunch, a friend and I discussed what I wanted to do with my life. I struggled to think for myself. I had lost my self-confidence and the self-belief that I amounted to something. Growing up, everyone thought I was determined. Now I felt lost, lonely and not enough. I was reminded that I had transferable skills. That evening, I came home, looked online, and found a job to apply for.

The job was at my old university, which I thoroughly loved, but the time spent there added more and more to my anxiety and depression. It looked like I was coming home again on paper, but in reality, this just added more unworthiness to my life.

Whilst working there, I met someone I knew when I was working as a lawyer. He was a personal development coach, and I attended a few of his programs. He was mighty proud to see a former student do so well. He didn't know that I was unhappy internally. I bit the bullet to tell him how much I felt like a failure. If I wasn't a failure, what was I? I was crying my eyes out as I still hadn't found my feet, and I was about to reach the big 40.

Once I decided to get to know myself honestly, warts and all, I had to face the music, and if I didn't like what I saw, I had to deal with it. I remember experiencing jealousy one Ramadan. I freaked out and messaged my Islamic scholar with sheer panic. I had never been jealous before, yet here I was in the holy month of Ramadan. I was referred to read Imam Ghazali's book on jealousy and follow it through. Later, whilst scrolling, I came across a Facebook post explaining how one is exposed to his faults so they can be worked on. For a believer, signs are everywhere, even on Facebook!

So, I decided to go deeper. Why was I jealous? I was not too fond of this feeling of being jealous. I was ready to let this go, so I hired a coach. I wanted to see my inner wisdom. I had a wealth of knowledge and life experience, yet I was an unhealthy empath without boundaries. I was co-dependent in every relationship and attracting narcissists was something

I specialised in. I was always drained, constantly exhausted and surrounded by negativity.

To my younger self, I am thankful to her for recognising she needed help. She stood up to heal the generational trauma that had been carried on for years. The first step is to set an intention to heal. This helps create hope and a desire to heal. But we must also recognise that when we are told actions are by intentions, they are interconnected. You must follow your intention with actions; otherwise, they are just wishes.

Healing took much work. The build-up leading to my healing took a long time. I was forever yoyoing. Healing was scary because it was unknown. Happy and sad seemed to be the primary emotions, and then anger and frustration would come along. But true healing came when I decided the desire for relief outweighed the fear of entering the unknown. The pain had become my comfort zone. I knew what to expect if I stayed here. But what did I value more?

I was ready to heal. I was sick of being on this rollercoaster. I had prayed for life to be over, and it never happened. I realised that I was meant to live. But I had to decide whether I would plod along in life or start living and loving life. I wanted a life worth living. I wanted a loving, fulfilling life. Healing was the price I had to pay for the life I wanted.

This time was different, and I knew I had to take action and change my life. I was frustrated by the repeating cycle, and there was a spark of hope to now change. There was a force within me that was ready to change. I felt motivated. Now was the time for me to heal. I decided to act now.

I knew I needed someone to help me, but who would this person be? I had had bad experiences from some of my previous attempts, and others had worked but I needed to go deeper, so I trusted my judgement, asked Allah for guidance and booked myself in with someone I felt aligned with.

There was a light inside of me, and I felt happy and excited, knowing I was about to enter the greatest period of my life. Yes, I was apprehensive, financially and mentally. I had prayed for guidance and knew I had chosen the correct path. The power was not to resist fear but to lean into it and see what it wanted to protect me from. As I say to my clients, "fear is just false evidence appearing real, and you have to say, I do not have time for this right now." When you swim with the tide, you go far. This was the best decision I made. As I gained clarity, the soul purpose I sought became clear. I had found my calling.

Once healed, I spoke to my work coach, who had given me some advice previously. I decided to share my news with him as I no longer felt like a failure. I had found my life passion. He said," I think of you often, but I never worry about you. I knew you would find your calling. I remember you telling me about how you did x, y and z; your eyes shone, and your soul lit up. I knew you would ring me up one day, and we would have this conversation." He told me to keep him updated with my progression as he would love to see my growth, and more than anything, he was happy to see me truly happy from the deepest depth of my soul. At age 40, I found myself.

I love the woman I have become — a woman who can use her unconscious mind to reveal what is bothering her deeply. I love bartering with it and finding guidance. Having healed from my past, I now see growth opportunities. I can now see when I am projecting or when something is being projected on me. My emotions are regulated now, so I no longer suppress or explode if something comes up. I have changed internally and externally. I am doing the things I once loved, but this time it is deeper. I am healthier and wealthier in all aspects of my life. Life has thrown a few curveballs along the way, and I think Allah was testing my commitment to the process.

During these tests, I put my blinkers on, focused on my goals, and trained as a master practitioner and trainer of NLP, Hypnotherapy, and Time Line Resourcing. I decided to launch my training academy. Nothing was stopping me. I took imperfect action and carried on working towards my goals and the next version of me. I often remind myself that I am a gardener and must tend to my garden. Sometimes a weed or two creeps in, but I know what to do. When Muslims arrived in Gibraltar before moving onto Andalusia, they burnt all their boats, so there was no way back. This was my moment. Was I committed to becoming a pro coach? Was I ready to burn my boats? The answer is YES! Every morning I wake up, and after takbeer, my first thought is; I am a pro coach. As I mentioned before, I then ask, "am I growing or dying?" and resoundingly, the response is, I am growing. Creating this space creates more time to live my dreams and coach fearlessly.

Growth is often compounded and realised into fruition quickly, and that's exactly what it felt like for me. Within days of becoming a multi-certified coach, I created and shared this movement in the world. A pre-launch countdown had begun. Two days before my launch day, I got my first client. She mentioned she had been considering the NLP course alongside her other reflective practises she was partaking in and said, 'I want you to be my coach'. I was amazed. Alhamdullilah, how blessed I was. Many coaches did not have paid clients for the first six months, and I had a client before my launch day. This wasn't about coaching; it was about finding my soul purpose.

I had organised a virtual launch party as it was during the pandemic. I had chosen my favourite day in the year, 11th November, for my launch date – 11:11. My first client had also paid for her session on that day. I was on cloud nine. Everything was perfectly aligned. The morning was spent with friends and mentors, and the evening was with my family. I had invited my Ustadah to an online gathering. I asked her if she recalled when I was suffering from anxiety and depression, and she had advised me to go into Khidmah (service) with the women in my community. At the time, it made no sense to me. My Ustadah replied with her favourite word, 'ah miskeen' and told me there was barakah (blessings) in what I was doing. At that moment, I recalled the dream of a teacher who I had told that I wanted to do holistic healing a long time before I even began coaching. And here I was, doing just that. I messaged my teacher, whom we lovingly call the Oracle and told him of my new business. He responded with, "ma'sha'Allah, stay focused". I was truly blessed to be here, considering a few years back, I was tired of life. All my sources of inspiration were behind me, and more importantly, I was behind me. For once, I knew what I wanted to do.

I was excited. I had my first client session on the week of my launch. What a blessing that was. My client had a paradigm shift. At that moment, she saw white birds flying. To this day, this has become her anchor. She often sends me videos of birds flying as a sign of her elevation and growth. She recently visited the holy land and sent me a clip of birds flying. She is flying in all she does, and may she continue to do so.

As I continued to coach, an old client returned. A particular client reached out as she felt stuck due to her money mindset. We had worked on this previously, and her business had flourished. Immediately, my intuition knew this was not the case this time. The presenting problems indicated another area of her life; relationships. I asked powerful coaching questions to trigger and activate her unconscious mind to reveal the root cause, which was precisely as I felt. Remember always to trust your gut! The decision was hers; did she want to heal from this area of her life or continue in this cycle?

Fortunately for her, she took the path of healing and transforming.

Another client wanted a deep transformation that consisted of my unique conscious coaching style. She informed me that she was struggling financially and only wanted a few sessions. If you coach like a pro, the clients get the desired results. And she did. I often laugh with her and say she had an absolute determination to heal. At the end of our time working together, she told me she had been on the verge of divorcing her husband when she had come to me, and now fast forward three months, and she was trying for another baby with him. Now, this was a happy ending I liked.

To cater for women who were not able or ready to invest in coaching, I created a what's app group. There were only two conditions; that you were female and deeply desired change. Women came from all over the world to surround themself with those who would empower, encourage and be a part of their growth. We started with Mental Health January, Self-love February, and Wellness March; after a break for Ramadan, we had 'find your soul purpose' and so on. I coached fearlessly from that space, and more and more clients were transforming.

My workshops focused on self-love and essence (fitra). I was truly humbled. A delegate had come with very low self-esteem. She was broken and had nothing good to say about herself. At the end of the session, she was crying tears of gratitude. She was in awe of herself as she now saw herself as a gift from Allah. This aligned with my intentions, and I was grateful to see it manifest.

Alongside workshops, I delivered an 8-week growth program at a local college for 16-18 years. The students had many needs, all of which I addressed. Once a week, I turned up and delivered an interactive workshop. I noticed the changes in the students. The beauty was that they also started to recognise these changes, and one student even surprised those around him. Only a few people were aware of the growth program, yet everyone noticed that this student was now very confident for someone who barely spoke. When asked why, he advised that the program had given him the skills to empower himself, and he was able to let go of things and make space for things that mattered.

During Ramadan, I also delivered a workshop on finding your soul purpose for Her Majesty's Court and Tribunal Service. It was open to non-Muslims to combat Islamophobia. One delegate said she had expected another dry talk from another Muslim woman, yet she found this fascinating. She did not realise that Islam gave so much scope to discovering oneself. This was an essential principle of Islam: to know Allah, one must know oneself. Another delegate found the practical tips to actualise her potential and attain personal goals very helpful.

Later that year, I also delivered a workshop on managing stress and anxiety, and this was such a success that the organiser asked me to come again. A delegate, whom I had coached after the first workshop, brought her cousin. She wanted her cousin to see me in action. I had helped the original delegate, and after three sessions, she said she had found a better version of herself. Her cousin signed up for a breakthrough, and by the end of that, her life had changed. A young girl, unable to express herself, was now fully ready to enter the next chapter of her life; she was getting married.

And that is how I have now empowered and coached over 100 women to find their true purpose and live the life they desire, and the beautiful realisation for me is that this is just the beginning.

Everyone around me already knew this was my calling. It was time for me to see. I couldn't see this before, as my trauma and pain blinded me. Once I healed, I saw how unauthentic I had been and how out of alignment with what my soul desired.

Knowing my true identity allowed me to live the life I once dreamed of. I gained freedom, peace of mind and a zeal for life. I was one step closer to the next version of me, living my soul purpose with true love, healing and spirituality. These were no longer labels but my core identity. My intuition guided me; now, I felt, saw, and heard clearly what I wanted and where I wanted to go.

Intentions are powerful when followed by actions; otherwise, they are mere wishes. Everything is created from within before it manifests outwards, good or bad. This is why great sages like Mawlana Rumi tell you to look within. You can dream, visualise, and wish all day long. You can read and obtain information. Information becomes knowledge when you transform it with action.

Every person has a choice: to stay where they are or to take the inward journey to purify their soul. Are you willing to release the trauma so you can start living the life of your dreams? Only you are responsible for life. You decide if you want to take action or stay in the circumstances.

Allah has made each and every one of us powerful. To change, a person has to change internally, and their environment must match their growth. If not, it will stunt them. The question is, are you ready to get the resources and take action to become the most powerful version of yourself?

About the Author
UMM SADIQ

Umm Sadiq is an experienced certified and accredited Master Coach, an internationally recognised NLP Master Practitioner and a hypnotherapist. She is also a trainer in NLP, Time

Line Resourcing®, Hypnosis and Conscious Coaching.

Umm Sadiq is currently working towards being a Master Trainer of NLP, which is the highest recognised qualification in this field.

She has developed her unique coaching style from years of practice in servitude, a student of knowledge and personal growth. The foundation is to know oneself to expand one's level of consciousness to, in turn, expand one's God Consciousness.

She has helped many women who were stuck spiritually, mentally, physically and emotionally. They transformed their lives by mastering their emotions and healing from their past, allowing them to feel and enjoy living a life that fulfils their dreams.

Before starting her coaching business, Umm Sadiq spent many years working as a lawyer, gaining sacred knowledge and specialising in pro bono and pastoral care.

After a successful career, she put her life experience into coaching as a tool to purify the soul. Umm Sadiq is now helping women love themselves, practice self-compassion and find peace within to reconnect with their Creator and core self (Fitra).

Umm Sadiq created her business, Conscious 11, after years of seeking something that would include everything she once needed to heal and find inner peace. She travelled near and far before she healed, searching for peace. Now she wants you to experience the same mindset shift so you can finally live intentionally and purposefully – a contentment-filled life.

Umm Sadiq enjoys travelling, creating memories and experiences, archery, running, managing a small property rental business and fundraising.

You can reach Umm Sadiq at:

Email address   admin@conscious11.com

facebook.com/consciouseleven
instagram.com/consciouseleven
linkedin.com/in/Umm%20Sadiq